EX LIBRIS

A SUSSEX GUIDE

SUSSEX WILDLIFE

DAVID MORTIMER

INTRODUCED BY
DR TONY WHITBREAD

Illustrated by
HUGH RIBBANS

SNAKE RIVER PRESS

SNAKE RIVER PRESS

Book No 10
Books about Sussex for the enthusiast

Published in 2008 by
SNAKE RIVER PRESS
South Downs Way, Alfriston, Sussex BN26 5XW
www.snakeriverpress.co.uk

ISBN 978-1-906022-09-9

This book was conceived, designed and produced by
SNAKE RIVER PRESS

Copyright © Snake River Press Limited 2008
Text © David Mortimer
Illustration © Hugh Ribbans

ART DIRECTOR & PUBLISHER *Peter Bridgewater*
EDITORIAL DIRECTOR *Viv Croot*
EDITOR *Robert Yarham*
PAGE MAKEUP *Richard Constable & Chris Morris*
ILLUSTRATOR *Hugh Ribbans*
CONSULTANT *Lorraine Harrison*

This book is typeset in Perpetua & Gill Sans,
two fonts designed by Eric Gill

Printed and bound in China

DEDICATION

To Sheila for her interest and patience;
and to Mark, for his uncomplaining help and encouragement.

CONTENTS

FOREWORD

I am not a native of Sussex. I first came here early in 1987 having hardly even visited beforehand. My perception then was miles away from reality. A small area just south of London surely could not have much of value to anyone interested in ecology. And this from someone who was born in Essex!

How wrong could one person be? Short term contracts with the then Nature Conservancy Council eventually were replaced by a permanent job with the Sussex Wildlife Trust. Along the way I was very fortunate to have picked up some experience of ecological surveys. My job has also given me the great privilege of meeting both expert natural historians and other enthusiastic people who just have a love for the wild places of Sussex. My superficial and incorrect view of Sussex changed after just a few minutes in the county and in the following two decades I have found, unsurprisingly, that there is always more that you can learn.

Sussex's natural variety works at all scales. You could look north from Ditchling Beacon and 'read' how the habitats fit the geology and topography of the landscape. You can walk through Ashdown Forest and enjoy the wide expanse of heathland. You can go to individual sites that can inspire and stimulate interest, and at a smaller scale, I know of people who have spent years studying the insects in an alleyway next to their house. Patrick Roper, one of the best naturalists in the county, has also committed to spending a large part of his life observing all life in just one square metre of his garden!

It is this very diversity that makes Sussex so special. Ecologists often worry about landscape fragmentation – how isolated woods, grassland, wetlands or heathlands are from each other. If habitats are isolated, wildlife cannot move in and out of them and survive; habitats will degrade and the landscape will lose variety. This is all the more tant with the environmental changes that are likely to hit us as a result of climate change. But the variety of Sussex means that habitats are not as isolated as they are, for example, in the Midlands or East Anglia. Though 'de-fragmenting' our landscape – re-building the links between habitats – is still vital, at least we are building on one of the strengths of the county.

One down side of the great natural variety of Sussex is that it is very difficult to choose just 20 favourite places. If I had to choose 20 my list would probably not look so very different from David Mortimer's. But how would you keep it to 20? Also I would always be tempted to add in extra bits around the edges of the ones I select and, before you know it, all my favourite sites would have joined up to form an interconnected network covering the whole county. Maybe that is the point, and perhaps this book could be read in that light. The 20 special places could be seen as exceptional 'nodes' within a much wider matrix of interconnecting high-quality wildlife sites. You could enjoy these 20, get to know other special places, small or large, or get to know the matrix that makes up the green backcloth of Sussex within which these outstanding places sit. Whatever you decide, the journey will be as good as the getting there!

DR TONY WHITBREAD
Chief Executive, Sussex Wildlife Trust

INTRODUCTION

*'We need to keep in touch with the wild, not for the sake of the world,
but in order to keep in touch with our own sanity.'*
SIMON BARNES

We who live in Sussex are singularly fortunate. We know we live in one of England's most beautiful counties. Despite the splashes of concrete and the efforts of politicians to enlarge them, the evidence is plainly visible every time we make a journey from west to east or vice versa. If we stop to consider the rich diversity through which we are passing, Sussex becomes an even more blessed plot. Almost instinctively, the name conjures a mental picture, maybe of the South Downs, rolling grasslands atop chalk cliffs; or perhaps of the open heaths and scattered pines of Ashdown Forest; or, yet again, of networks of small fields fringed by rews, shaws or hedges. But, as a matter of hard fact, it is woodlands, many of them ancient, that are the true hallmark of the county, which is one of the most highly wooded in England.

A Sussex man, Gideon Mantell, from Lewes, plotted the underlying geology in *The Geology of the South-East of England*, published in 1827. Between Surrey's North Downs and our own South Downs, Weald clay overlays beds of freshwater limestone, broken in the north of the county by elevated ridges of sandstone (in which Mantell found the world's first fossils of dinosaurs). Weald clay is good for trees but poor for agriculture, so whilst our forebears busied themselves with clearing much of England's woodland, they tended to leave it in place in Sussex. Seventy per cent of the Weald was still wooded at the time of the *Domesday Book*, and almost a millennium later, at the opening of the 21st century, 14.5 per cent of it still is, against a national average of 2.6 per cent.

The combination of wealden forest and sandstone ridges gave us further diversity in the form of narrow ghylls, many of them surprisingly deep, as erosion washed out the clay between the lines of sandstone some ten thousand years ago. And our ancestors, from the Romans to the men of Tudor times, were quick to see the possibility of rocks bearing iron ore. However improbable it may seem to us now, Sussex was the industrial heart of the nation in the 16th and 17th centuries, with the deafening sounds of hammer mills polluting the countryside for miles around, and the heat and noise of England's first blast furnaces echoing through many a ghyll. Large areas of Sussex enjoy a tranquillity today that was unknown to them 500 years ago, but the legacy that remains includes the many ponds that were created to provide the water to drive the mills.

The county's diversity is extended as the chalk hills of the Downs come into view, for in several places – behind Pevensey or between Amberley and Pulborough, for example – there are levels intercut by streams that are still prone to flooding despite their drainage ditches. And notwithstanding the demands of agriculture, the Downs them-selves provide acres of chalk grasslands and even, in one or two places, of rare chalk heath. Add to all this the variations in climate encountered on either side of the Downs and it is easy to see why Sussex has such a wealth of wildlife habitats – a wealth enhanced by our proximity to the Continent, and the migratory birds, beetles and butterflies that reach us from that direction.

Climate change & Sussex wildlife

Climate change is one of the world's hot topics in these early years of the 21st century. Whatever the underlying cause there is no denying the fact of it, and the effect has been likened to the British Isles sailing southwards at the rate of 45 miles in every decade. As with any change the outcome can be beneficial in some directions and harmful in others. Bewl Water, on the borders of East Sussex and Kent, is an attractive habitat for great crested and little grebes, but as the water levels fell to dangerously low levels in the 18 months of near drought between early 2005 and September 2006, the numbers of both these birds fell right away during the breeding season. In 2005, for example, only one pair of great crested grebes successfully produced young.

On the other hand, warmer temperatures can attract species that either shunned us as a damp, foggy island, or departed at high speed when winter approached. In recent times, species new to Britain have begun to call in; in other cases visitors have been able to linger longer or stay to establish colonies, and in this respect Sussex has been especially fortunate thanks to its favourable climate and the diversity of its habitats. In the past few years gardeners have noticed that many flowers are blooming later and later in the year. So too are butterflies, such as the red admiral, numbers of which were seen on the wing and feeding in Sussex in December 2006. The intriguing hummingbird hawk moth that, like its avian namesake, hovers as it feeds, has been breeding here for 30 years but, until recently, winter regularly killed off its progeny. Now it seems to be surviving in some quantity and was seen on the wing in February 2007. The spectacular black- and yellow-hooped wasp spider is enjoying similar success. This is our largest spider and spins its web over hollows in chalk downland to trap its grasshopper prey. It first appeared in this country in 1922 but, needing warm summers and mild winters, has only begun to flourish and multiply in recent years.

Managing reserves

Sussex boasts a high number of areas attractive to wildlife, many of which – but by no means all – are protected reserves. Because of the county's diversity these reserves vary greatly in type of habitat. Moreover the wealden pattern of farming, characterised by small fields with rews and shaws connecting wooded areas, gives our mammals, birds and insects more cover under which to move about than they would enjoy in many other parts of the country. Nevertheless, reserves are a little like islands, and just as many migrants come to Britain supposing the grass to be greener here, so wildlife takes advantage of a reserve where the food supply suits it until overcrowding begins to damage the very conditions that attracted it in the first place. And so wildlife reserves have to be managed at both the macro and micro levels.

Strategic decisions have to be taken. Is this or that reserve attractive to these or those endangered species and, if so, what food chains need to be encouraged or protected? If this or that plant, bird, insect or animal flourishes here, will it be at the expense of others that might be of equal value? And so on. And once the strategic decisions have been taken the micro-management is continual. In one sense, a wildlife reserve is not a garden, tended to be pretty and manicured in all seasons. In another it may be exactly like a garden, needing continual care and maintenance, weeding as it were, to achieve the conditions that are right. It is remarkable just how quickly the unchecked growth of nature can overrun an area if left to its own devices. To take a single example, an area of field or heath, if left ungrazed by cattle or untended by volunteers can become thick with bramble and birch or dogwood scrub in what seems like no time. You may enjoy the beauties of this or that reserve, assuming it is untouched by human hand but, in almost every case, the opposite is so.

Selecting 20 wildlife reserves for this book has been far from easy. I have attempted to ensure an even spread across the county, to shadow in my choice the same diversity that Sussex enjoys and, of course, to select only sites that have open public access. Even so, there may be favourites (and there are one or two of my own) that are not here, and if that is the case I can only apologise and plead author's privilege!

I must disclaim any pretence of being a lifelong countryman, let alone a professional botanist or zoologist. I have written as an enthusiastic layman with a small degree of knowledge, acquired from those who know better than me, and from listening and observing whenever possible. I have not written for experts but for other laymen who, like me, treasure the myriad natural wonders, many of them well hidden, to be found deep in the beautiful Sussex countryside – and especially the flora and fauna that flourish within them, from courting adders and shy bitterns to unusual butterflies and spectacular wild flowers. If I persuade you to visit a wildlife reserve you do not know, I will be rewarded. If you come away from it sharing my own enthusiasm, I will indeed have succeeded in my aim.

Many people think that conservation is just about saving fluffy animals – what they don't realise is that we're trying to prevent the human race from committing suicide.

GERALD DURRELL

KINGLEY VALE

ANCIENT YEWS & SUNLIT GRASS

Kingley Vale is no ordinary place. Whether or not it is your first visit, your awareness seems heightened by its aura and you sense a tingle in your nerve ends. As you approach it along the signed ten-minute walk from the car park, you get little inkling of what awaits you. You have the impression of a deciduous wood on the same level as the fields around you, and when the trees are in leaf there is no hint of the combe that lies behind it or of the steep ridge of Bow Hill. Yet you are about to enter a site that almost certainly contains the oldest living things in Britain, a place that bears evidence of human activity from the Stone Age to the present day.

This is the only National Nature Reserve in West Sussex. A circular trail is clearly marked around it, and given a choice of going straight ahead or to the left the first option is recommended. You will not have gone far before you become aware of the yew trees on your right – and these are no ordinary trees but huge, age-twisted yews, riven over the centuries by storms and tempests. Yews are almost impossible to date and conjectures about their age range from 500 to 2000 years old, but the most probable guess would put them between 500 and 800 years old. The naturalist W. H. Hudson wrote of them as

dark religious trees with trunks like huge, rudely fashioned pillars of red and purple ironstone. One has the sensation of being in a vast cathedral.

The sense of awe engendered by these ancient living things is unimpaired, and it needs little imagination to understand why our distant ancestors thought such forests haunted and frightening. One of the many legends asserts that Kingley Vale was the site of a battle in 895 AD between Viking Danes, who put ashore to plunder as they fled along the coast from defeat at Exeter, and the men of Chichester, who soundly defeated them. The encounter was real enough and is recorded in the *Anglo-Saxon Chronicle*, but whether Kingley Vale was the site of it is another matter. When at last you can tear yourself away from these mighty trees, you continue through glades where oak and ash flourish until you emerge, suddenly it seems, onto the lower slopes of the combe and its close-cropped chalk grassland. Over the centuries these downland slopes have been grazed by countless generations of sheep, and though their descendants are not currently at work, the rabbits and deer are making up for their absence. Indeed, there are now so many deer that they are starting to cause harm and the habitat is undergoing change. There is a scattering of roe deer in the reserve and the shy little muntjac has been seen, but fallow deer rule here. A herd of about 50 does with their fawns spends most of the year in the Vale, going out at night to browse surrounding farmland, and the number swells to around 100 when the bucks gather for the rutting season in October. If, then, you were among the ancient yews in the fading light and heard far off the unearthly 'groaning belch' of the males, you could understand the fear of unseen spirit or animal danger our distant ancestors had. Richard Williamson, who has monitored and cared for Kingley Vale for 40 years, wrote memorably of

> *a sound I had never heard before…a black sound full of our dark memories of the night forest; it was the intangible emotion of an animal.*

The grazing of the growing numbers of deer in the reserve is reducing the undergrowth on which some species of bird, once common here, depend for their livelihood. Birds have been regularly monitored for 40 years and are showing a gradual decline in numbers and species – though not, thankfully, blackbirds, robins and chaffinches. On the other hand, the redwings and fieldfares that migrate from Europe are now less often seen and the flocks of thrushes that gather to feed on wintertime seeds and berries are smaller than they used to be. But you will still hear the cat-like mew of buzzards, and may well catch a glimpse of kestrels, hobbies and sparrowhawks, or the owl that produces the classic tu-whit-tu-whoo call, the tawny.

But let us return to the sunlit grassland. Here, regular grazing has the effect of checking the growth of those plants and flowers with an inclination to dominate and crowd out others. This has allowed a great variety of species to flourish, as many as 300, including rockrose, eyebright, wild thyme, bird's foot trefoil, harebell and clustered bellflower; and two rarities, the least flowered buttercup (*Ranunculus parvi flora*) and the hairy violet (*Viola hirta*). Also among Kingley Vale's treasures is the range of orchids to be seen, such as the early purple, common spotted, butterfly, bee, fly, frog, fragrant, pyramid – and one meriting special mention, the endangered narrow-leaved heleborine (*Cephalanthera longjfolia*). The last appears only occasionally in the vale, but as it has been lost at several of its few sites elsewhere in the country, any appearance is to be warmly welcomed, the more so as it is unusually elegant, even for an orchid. Over a foot tall, its favoured habitat is close to beeches growing on chalk, and it blossoms in May and June bearing up to 40 pure white flowers standing clear and proud of the stem above long, slender leaves.

Like the birds and the plants, the butterflies too are closely monitored and recorded, and of the 58 species known to breed in Britain, 39 are found in Kingley Vale, more than on any of the other 200 National Nature Reserves in Britain. Among the results of regular recording is the recognition of an eight-year cycle exhibiting a 'sawtooth' graph – increase followed by decrease, followed by increase, then decrease again, etc. This pattern is the same all over the country on sites where management is stable. All very well, you may be muttering, but what can I actually see? With 39 breeding species the answer, clearly, is plenty but it is well worth looking out for grizzled skippers, of which there are good colonies; for holly blues and for the chalkhill blues that rely on the horseshoe vetch that grows here. There are marbled whites and brown arguses, two species that cannot exist on agriculturally improved grassland and, in sunlit patches among the trees, you may see speckled woods dancing or fighting.

As the slope steepens you become conscious of being enclosed within the horns of a bow (possibly giving its name to the hill), the flanks of which are densely clothed with dark yews. Westward they are interspersed with the lighter green of deciduous trees, spectacularly so in spring, but eastward, in the direction the trail takes you, they are almost unbroken. These are younger than their mighty ancestors below, but as you climb through them you are struck by the apparently lifeless gloom deep within. Yet what better place for fallow deer to lie up by day, where their acute smell and hearing can detect everything without the distraction of extraneous noise?

Suddenly you are above the trees and out onto Bow Hill, a long, curved ridge of untold, mysterious antiquity that modern archaeologists have yet – if ever – to unravel. Throughout the reserve, on the ridge and in the vale, are 16 sites of importance (including bell and bowl barrows) from the mid-Stone Age to the Bronze Age. The collapsed domes of the two biggest and best-known, both Bronze Age, show where amateur 18th- and 19th-century diggers hoped to recover buried treasure rather than the burnt bones that were their reward. But if antiquity fails to excite you, your compensations are the views north, south and east. Chichester cathedral appears like a galleon making its stately westward way to the inlets of Chichester harbour in which, in your mind's eye, you might see the longboats of Vikings sailing in towards their bloody destiny long before ever a cathedral rose above the surrounding houses.

Getting there   National grid ref. SU821103
🜂 A286 Chichester-Midhurst road to East Lavant; turn west through West Stoke;
  follow brown National Nature Reserve signpost (on tricky bend).

Seasonal highlights
🍃 *Spring*: wild flowers and early orchids; birds.
🍃 *Summer*: later orchids; butterflies.
🍃 *Autumn*: butterflies; fallow deer gathering.
🍃 *Winter*: winter birds.
🍃 *All seasons*: the ancient yews and the views from Bow Hill.

IPING & STEDHAM COMMONS

TWO IN ONE

W hat could be better – two for the price of one! Despite their different names, Iping and Stedham commons sit side by side, served by a common car park, and are prime examples of an endangered habitat, dry lowland heath. Once, such heathland stretched across Sussex and Hampshire, and on into Dorset. Today, over 80 per cent of it has been lost to agriculture and forestry and only by careful and continuous management can the remaining heathland continue to support the uncommon wildlife that depends upon it for survival. But before we mutter darkly to ourselves about man's heedless waste, it is as well to remember that most heath is itself the result of woodlands on mineral soils being cleared for grazing long ago.

For centuries, villagers and smallholders grazed their cattle on the heath forcing them – since bell heather, ling and gorse thrive on the dry sandy conditions to the exclusion of most types of grass – to live off the shoots of would-be trees and shrubs. As common land grazing died out with the development of modern living, invaders were quick to move in, the ever-eager birch tree in the vanguard. By the time Iping and Stedham became nature reserves, much hard labour lay ahead to clear the birch scrub and restore the open vistas characteristic of heathland. Much of the scrub has to be hand-pulled, for just below the surface of the soil a birch sapling has a rosette of buds only too willing to throw out multiple stems if the main one is cut. Luckily, heather seeds remain dormant for up to half a century and the reward for those toiling to clear the ground is the speed with which they germinate once light is restored. So summertime visitors to Iping and Stedham may once more be greeted by gently undulating banks of crimson-purple.

Human visitors are not the only beneficiaries. The little silver-studded blue butterfly (*Plebeius argus*) adores bell heather and, between mid-June and early July, clouds of them can be seen fluttering above it – like 'blue confetti', it has been said. If this tiny butterfly, less than an inch long, sits still long enough for you to observe it, its name becomes self-evident. The male is a brilliant blue, and the underside of its wings is fringed with black and orange spots enclosed in silvery-white circles. By contrast, the female is a rather drab brown with less prominent 'studs'. The silver-studded blue has a remarkable symbiotic relationship with a species of black ant living on the Commons. Its larvae are taken into the ants' nests throughout their winter development providing, in return, a sweet liquid from tiny glands. The caterpillar emerges around March to browse the bell heather, but even then is free to return to the ants' nest for protection from parasitic wasps as it turns into the chrysalis from which, in June, the butterfly appears in all its glory.

Digger and sand wasps are among an army of insects at home in the dry, acidic soil of the heath. If you inspect the low sandy banks you may find a small hole leading into the burrow of one of these parasitic wasps and, given patience and luck, you might even see one dragging a para-lysed moth caterpillar inside for its grubs to feed on. But the sand wasp in its turn may fall prey to a distant cousin, the ruby tail wasp, and find itself on the receiving end of similar treatment. The green tiger beetle (*Cicindela campestris*) has been called 'one of the most glamorous British insects', and it is another that finds heathland an ideal habitat. You are more than likely to see a green blur as one hums past, but if it comes to rest you will be struck by the brilliance of its green wing cases, spotted with yellow. A really close inspection reveals fearsome mandibles as among insects this is a top predator, feeding voraciously on ants and small insects. Tiger beetles also create burrows for their larvae, but with a difference. They make a hole into which a single larva fits very

snugly, tail down, with only its head protruding above the surface ready
to snap up any passing ant or other food, and as there are something
like 5000 different kinds of invertebrate living on these heaths, a choice
of nutrition is usually within reach of an eager mandible. A static
carnivore is also resident at Stedham, around the edges of the black,
peaty pools on the southern side. The round-leaved and oblong-leaved
sundews put out leaves covered in tendrils exuding sticky globules of
great interest to unwary insects that are caught on them, then slowly
devoured to supplement the low nutrients the plant receives from
the acidic soil.

Sharing top spot as a predator with the tiger beetle is an insect in
plentiful supply on Iping Common that, in human eyes, is among the
unlikeliest of fierce hunters. The dragonfly beguiles us with its short-
lived beauty and the way it seems to shimmer in flight as sunlight catches
its dazzling colours. Can this delicate creature really be the scourge of
so many fellow insects? It can, and like the tiger beetle, it is formidably
armed. Not only does it have powerful jaws, but the inside of its legs carry
thorn-like serrations for gripping prey. If you want simply to admire
the beauty of dragonflies and damselflies, make for a largish pond on
the northern edge of Iping Common, especially in August. The pond is
just inside the boundary with the A272, screened by trees and shrubs on
its eastern and northern flanks. On a bright, sunny day there are scores
of black darter, southern hawker and migrant hawker dragonflies and
small red-eyed damselflies mating or making mating flights. The small
red-eyed damselfly (*Erythromma viridulum*) is distinguished by its bright
powder-blue body and, as the name implies, prominent red eyes. It was
unknown in Britain until 1999 but, possibly because of the rise in average
annual temperatures, has become the first example of a migrant damselfly
settling down here to breed and create colonies.

The gorse bushes that distinguish Iping and Stedham provide the
habitat beloved of another comparative rarity, the Dartford warbler
(*Sylvia undata*). This shy little bird nests deep inside the gorse, protected
by its sharp thorns, with its favourite food – spiders – in plentiful supply
amongst the dense mass of the plant. Bad winters are, literally, death

to Dartford warblers and the freezing months of early 1963 reduced their numbers to 12 pairs in the whole of Britain. They have recovered since, but the scarcity of heathland still makes this warbler a prize to be valued should you see it flitting above the bushes with much flapping of wing and wagging of tail. Best of all is a summer visitor – the nightjar (*Caprimulgus Europaeus*). It feeds at dusk and dawn, taking insects on the wing and, since it is beautifully camouflaged when nesting on the ground, this is the best time to see – and hear – it. Its churring call is like the purring of a giant cat, and its aerial acrobatics are spectacular.

Of all the pleasures of this expansive reserve perhaps the greatest is the simplest – open vistas of gently rolling heath, especially so on Iping, where there are fewer trees as well as a small cluster of Bronze Age burial mounds. Stedham, by contrast, has two large stands of pine on its shallow backbone ridge and if you leave the paths you will find pits and scrapes remaining from the wartime training of Canadian troops. Sand lizards are plentiful on both Commons, as are slow worms and adders – and maybe, just maybe, the rarest and least seen of all British snakes lurks here, the smooth snake (*Coronella austriaca*). Not only is it rare, it is also cautious and secretive. Nevertheless, lizards and slow worms are its favourite food and heath its favourite habitat so the conditions are right. If, therefore, you see a snake about 2 feet (60 cm) long, with a narrower head than an adder and a continuous black stripe running through the eye and along the flank, contact the Sussex Wildlife Trust (*see p. 93*) as soon as possible!

Getting there   National grid ref. SU849221

❯ Take A272 heading west from Midhurst. Turn south on minor road
   signposted Elsted; car park is on right, 220 yards (200 m) after turning off A272.

Seasonal highlights

◄ **Spring**: *lizards, slow worms and adders; the mating displays of woodlark and Dartford warblers.*

◄ **Summer**: *heathers and ling; butterflies; dragonflies; the song of reintroduced field crickets; nightjars.*

◄ **Autumn**: *birds and (especially on Stedham) fungi.*

◄ **Winter**: *open vistas of heath; occasional sightings of hen harriers and great grey shrike.*

PAGHAM HARBOUR

WADERS & WATER VOLES

Mention Pagham Harbour and the instinctive reaction is shorebirds. To be sure, the variety and numbers of winter waders and wildfowl can delight a specialist and fascinate an interested layman. But this is a big reserve, covering 1500 acres (600 hectares), of which only half consists of salt flats and seawater, and if there is a single word that sums up the whole it is diversity. Wood-lands, meadows, hedgerows and reedbeds surround the saline lagoons, shingle and salt marshes of the ancient harbour, providing ideal con-ditions for a wealth of wild flowers, butterflies, dragonflies, moths and small mammals in addition to the birds. The visitor centre south of Sidlesham, on the western flank of the reserve, sells a useful colour-coded map detailing all the footpaths and the differing habitats that comprise Pagham Harbour.

In early medieval times Pagham's natural harbour was among the most important in the land, but by the beginning of the 14th century it was in decline. Recurrent storms narrowed the harbour mouth and allowed silt to accumulate behind it, rendering it increasingly useless as a port. In 1873 parliament decreed the sealing of its mouth so the land could be converted for farming, but mankind's hubris was short-lived. In 1910 the sea swept over the land and reclaimed its own in the biggest storm in memory. By 1964 the area had become a nature reserve recognised as a wetland of international importance.

From Pagham in the east and Church Norton in the west two shingle spits reach out like arms enfolding the harbour. A line of houses stretches along the eastern shingle to the car park, and you quickly realise that this spit is less commanding than its opposite number to the west. It is another reminder of the powerful vagaries of the sea. Latterly it has not been replenishing the Pagham spit as it used to. The sea has decided, for the time being at least, to deposit the shingle instead on the Church Norton spit which – to the delight of little terns and the superbly camouflaged ringed plovers that find it an ideal nesting site – is beginning to lower over its eastern neighbour.

Swept as it is by wind and salt spray the shingle is, remarkably, home to a variety of flowers. Almost inevitably, there are escapees from gardens on the Pagham side, and a profusion of valerian is beginning to cause a problem. But yellow horned poppy, sea kale, viper's bugloss, slender thistle and biting stonecrop are all at home on the shingle, mostly at their best in the first half of summer. One, however, childing pink, (*Petrorhagia nanteuilii*) is really special. Pagham Harbour is thought to be the only natural site of this attractive little June-flowering plant (although it has been artificially introduced in other places), and it is said to have the largest colony.

North and west of the harbour itself are reedbeds and damp, low-lying meadows forming part of the reserve (though the restored reedbed known as The Severals lies just outside its south-western boundary). These are habitats that have been declining in Britain for 60 years, thanks to changes in farming and flood control methods, putting at risk the life that traditionally flourished in them. Snipe are a good example, for nationally their numbers have fallen markedly, but they are birds that love wet meadows and you may spot one early in the year; should you fail, why not return in June to seek compensation in the southern marsh orchids. One animal in particular is thriving in the ditches and dykes around the damp meadows, despite suffering in recent years a countrywide fall in numbers approaching 90 per cent – the water vole (*Arvicola terrestris*), or Ratty of *The Wind in the Willows*. In fact, the water vole is not a rat and, if you manage to observe one, the immediate differences are its shorter, furry tail, its plumper body and its chubby face with a blunt, rounded nose that gives it a friendly, enquiring air. Part of its national decline came from changes in land use, but the major reason was the release of American mink from fur farms by unthinking protestors. These vicious predators came close to wiping out the water vole, but at Pagham careful monitoring has managed to free the area of mink and the recovery of water voles is a reward in which we can all delight.

For the avid birdwatcher there are three hides – near the Little Lagoon on Pagham Spit; near the Visitor Centre at Sidlesham; and at Glebe Meadow near Church Norton. For the first-time visitor there is a heart-stopping twice-daily experience. You may arrive when the tide is out, gaze at the broad expanse of salt flats, grey-green with the sea purslane that catches the silt and builds the mud levels, and think it all looks a trifle dull and featureless. The more poetic may appreciate the wide skies and subtle pastel shades and, from Church Norton, admire the distant view of Chichester Cathedral's spire against the backdrop of the South Downs, yet still feel vaguely disappointed; but return when the tide is up and it is impossible not to catch your breath at the trans-formation from a world of shifting mud pools and channels to one of rippling wavelets lapping the banks and coves. At such a moment the experience is almost spiritual.

It is these daily transformations that make the harbour a paradise for wildfowl. For the many different waders the receding sea exposes rich pickings in the mud flats, and the length of bill gives an instant clue to their respective diets. Shelduck and plovers, for example, have short beaks that pluck little hydrobia snails from the surface; redshank, knot and oystercatchers have longer beaks that probe for ragworms and corophium; and those with the longest bills, such as curlew and black-tailed godwit, whilst not averse to the worms and molluscs sought by shorter-beaked birds, are probing deep for lugworms and furrow shells.

Spring and autumn brings the migrants, passing through inwards or outwards and pausing for a few days to refuel from the rich diet before moving on. Among them there might be spoonbills, distinctive with their long white plumage trailing from the back of their heads and, as the name implies, long bills broadening into something resembling small, yellow-tipped shovels that they swish through the water to scoop up small fish and invertebrates. Or there might be the occasional red-throated or black-throated diver, flying south from its summer breeding grounds in the north of Scotland; or a green or purple sandpiper pausing on its inward or outward journey. In a large area like Pagham, full of rich pickings and varied habitats, you can never be sure when the next unusual visitor will drop in.

Of one thing you can be almost certain, however – that the winter months, from roughly November to March will bring hundreds, indeed thousands, of pintails, wigeon, teal, shelduck, oystercatcher, lapwing, plover, knot, dunlin, turnstone, redshank, godwit, curlew and brent geese. Among them may be merganser, goldeneye and grey heron and, in the summer months, whimbrel, common and sandwich tern, in addition to the little terns and little egrets that breed here. Little wonder that there are plans afoot to build a new, green, self-sustaining Coastal Centre on an old landfill site at the water's edge. But not even from its windows will you see into the reedbeds and spot the nests of the other prizes on the reserve – little grebes and great crested grebes. Some secrets are best kept.

Getting there   National grid ref. SZ856966

- ❯ Visitor Centre: take B2145 Chichester-Selsey road through
  Hunston and Sidlesham.
- ❯ Church Norton: continue past Visitor Centre and take first turning on left
  (about 2 miles, 3 km) Rectory Lane.
- ❯ Pagham Spit: take B2166 Chichester-Bognor Regis road, turn off at Pagham turn
  left down Sea Lane and at end take fourth exit off roundabout along Harbour Road.

Seasonal highlights

- *Spring*: waders and wildfowl; migrants passing through; early butterflies.
- *Summer*: butterflies, dragonflies and moths; shingle flowers; orchids.
- *Autumn*: migrants passing through; late butterflies and dragonflies.
- *Winter*: wintering waders and wildfowl; massed roosting flights of knot, etc.

LEVIN DOWN

HERDWICKS & BUTTERFLIES

Be warned! Levin Down is steep and although the footpaths mainly follow the contours of the hill on which it sits you need to bring reserves of stamina with you. Among the rewards for your endeavour are stunning views on all sides – but more of that later. The best starting point is from the crossroads in Charlton village. You have two choices: walk a few yards along the lane towards Singleton and take the clearly marked footpath across the upward-sloping field to enter the south-east corner of the Down; or walk the farm track northwards from the lay-by for just over half a mile (1 km) to enter the reserve at the north-east end, with a steep slope of hazel trees on your right as you do so, some with dormice boxes on them. At whatever point you enter you may see an occasional sheet of corrugated iron flat on the ground. This is not the result of fly-tipping, but a shelter for slow worms, and if you gently lift a corner you may find one or two dozing underneath. Slow worms are not snakes but legless lizards that are genial, uncomplaining characters and completely harmless (to humans).

Levin is a corruption of 'leave alone' and in the past Levin Down was known as Leave Alone Hill, which is a less-than-subtle hint as to how it became such a valued site for wildlife. It is the largest chalk heath in West Sussex, the light covering of grass made it poor grazing land for all but sheep, and at the same time well-nigh impossible to plough for crops thanks to its steepness and the chalk just below the surface.

surface. Other than for brief periods during World War II and in succeeding years, when cattle were invited to scratch around on it for whatever they could find to eat while the lower surrounding fields were ploughed to grow crops, Levin Down has been left as chalk grassland for centuries. That alone is uncommon these days, but there is something else that makes it a most unusual habitat. A few thousand years ago, during the last Ice Age, acid soils were blown in by the winds to mingle with the alkaline of the chalk, enabling us to enjoy the rare neighbouring of plants that require completely different soils in which to flourish, such as the ling heather and tormentil that grow side by side with thyme and marjoram.

There was a lengthy post-war period in which Levin Down went largely unnibbled by sheep, and scrub – never slow to take advantage of such gifts – began to close in, especially so on the south-facing slopes. It has taken many years of work by volunteers and contractors, recently joined for much of the year by Herdwicks – those hardy Lakeland sheep beloved of Beatrix Potter – to tip the balance back in favour of the plants whose true domain this is. This is not to say that all the scrub has been eradicated. Belts of hawthorn, buckthorn, spindle, dogwood, wild rose and omnipresent brambles are being left to create windbreaks and sheltered glades where butterflies flourish and certain birds, such as whitethroats and yellowhammers, can nest and entertain us with their songs. In the meantime the Herdwicks wander through these compartments, biting off the young bramble or dogwood shoots and preventing the glades closing in again. If you sit down for a while to enjoy the gorgeous views you may find yourself the centre of attention for a group of Herdwicks, wearing their trademark expression of faintly amused puzzlement. Do please keep your dog under control – in a recent year dogs killed two of these attractive sheep.

Thanks to the long work of scrub clearance, the wild flowers and the butterflies are once again the greatest of Levin's attractions. Cowslips are prolific and, on the lower slopes where the soil is that little bit richer, they grow tall, providing food for the rare Duke of Burgundy butterfly, whose caterpillars feed on it. Yet no sooner is that said than we come up against a conundrum. Just as the improvements to the site have allowed cowslips to proliferate, so sightings of this handsome butterfly with orange and black tracery on its large wings have dropped away to as little as one or two per season. Is this an effect of climate change? Are the cowslips now in bloom too early for it? Have the rabbits eaten the grass surrounding the cowslips and reduced the encircling shade that the butterflies require for their eggs? Nobody yet knows. With luck, it will prove to be a temporary blip, but thankfully there is no shortage of other butterflies competing for one's attention. Wild marjoram attracts many, such as the marbled white, and among the 35 different types here are also grizzled skippers, brown argus, yellow brimstones, green hairstreaks and, in September, brown hairstreaks can be seen performing their mating flights around their favourite ash trees.

Thanks to the unusual mix of soil types at Levin, and to the varying soil thicknesses at the top and bottom of the hill, there are subtle differences between the south- and east-facing slopes and at the different levels. Lower down amidst the longer grass, where you can see the best of the springtime cowslips, the beautiful clustered bellflowers show themselves off as summer draws towards its end. Nearer the top, where the grass is shorter, you will find salad burnet, wild thyme, fairy flax milkwort, carline thistle, quaking grass and autumn gentian crowding thickly together, cheek by jowl with the ling heather... and then there are the orchids. Common spotted orchids are everywhere – or so at least it seems when they reach their peak in June – but you may as easily see the pink spires of pyramidal orchids breaking through the lower growing wild flowers. However, the one for which you will have to search diligently in the autumn is the lady's tresses orchid, with its spiral of small white flowers which, unlike its showy cousins, is a mere 2 inches (5 cm) high.

On the south-facing slopes of Levin grows a downland plant that is becoming quite rare in England – wild juniper. It's having a battle to survive. At first it was in danger of being crowded out by freer-growing yew and scrub, but these encroachments have been largely dealt with.

Its other enemy – rabbits – provide a sterner test. As is all too apparent on these southern slopes, rabbits are causing major depredations on the hill, making it very difficult for juniper seedlings to establish themselves.

As for the views, you have only to look about you. From the south-facing slopes you look across a beautiful, tranquil valley to The Trundle, the hill to the immediate west of Goodwood racecourse crowning the ridge of Charlton Down. From the eastern slopes you look across to North Down, broken with scattered copses. But for a panorama to take the breath away keep climbing up through the reserve and out onto the pastureland that stretches across the dome of Levin Down. To the north, Charlton and Singleton forests stretch unbroken for miles along the hill-tops of the downs; and away to the west the ridges and hills appear to reach for the horizon. Apart from the village of Singleton far below, and a few scattered farmhouses, there are few signs of human habitation and there is only one significant road for miles around. The sense of timelessness is pervasive.

Yet there are more things to savour. Buzzards and kestrels are common enough around Levin Down but recently the red kite has spread here. In 2006 one pair nested in the vicinity and they seem to have bred successfully since, in 2007, three pairs of these handsome birds were noted, with their striking black and reddish-brown markings, their distinctive forked tails and effortless flight. If you are lucky enough to see them, you will be ready for the final delights – a downhill walk and a good pub – The Fox Goes Free – awaiting you at the bottom!

Getting there   National grid ref. SU885133
⦿ A286 Chichester to Midhurst road: turn east at Singleton village.
⦿ A285 Chichester to Petworth road: turn west along Droke Lane, through East Dean village.

Seasonal highlights
◂ *Spring: springtime wild flowers and early butterflies; dormice, adders, slow worms.*
◂ *Summer: orchids and wild flowers, the scent of wild thyme and butterflies.*
◂ *Autumn: autumn flowers and butterflies.*
◂ *Winter: the views, awe-inspiring in any season.*

EBERNOE COMMON

AN ENCHANTED FOREST

A Common it may be called, but this must be most people's childhood idyll of an enchanted forest. Even before you leave the small, unsurfaced car park by the tiny Victorian church, the unusual is there to delight or intrigue you. In April the little church-yard is awash with cowslips and bluebells, and in June with common spotted orchids. If your choice of path is to the right of the church, you will see outside the west end a small but poignant commemoration of two brothers and a girl who were killed in 1942 by a bomb, casually unloaded on nearby Petworth school by a German bomber as it returned from a raid on London. It stretches belief in so tranquil a spot, far removed from noise and bustle, let alone war

If you continue to the right of the church, you quickly drop down to Furnace Pond, its name a reminder of Sussex's industrial past, and take the south-westerly route into the forest. And a helpful hint before you start – the clearly marked paths round Ebernoe are few in number but run predominantly north-south. Should you lose your bearings, always head north to get back to the church and car park.

If, on the other hand, you take the bigger track to the left of the church you will pass Furnace Meadow, again to the left, a favourite haunt of adders. Tread softly because, unless it is early morning before their metabolisms have quickened in the warmth of the sun, they will hear you and flee long before you catch a glimpse of them.

If you carry on along the main track and take the left-hand path shortly after passing the cattle grid, Ebernoe reveals one of its sleeping secrets – a 300-year-old brick kiln that remained sporadically in use until 1930, and was restored in the early years of the 21st century using the same materials available to its original builders. Smallholders' cottages with evocative names like *Shottersland*, *Stokers Cottage* and *Golden Knob*, were once scattered throughout the forest, their owners growing what they could, and grazing their pigs on the beech mast. In the crevices of the old brick kiln, tiny pipistrelle bats make their homes – and bats are a clue to the greatest of Ebernoe's many glories; for it is the most important bat site in Britain, with 14 of the UK's 16 species roosting here. The holly that abounds in Ebernoe provides a stable, year-round, humid microclimate that some species of bat require, especially the rare barbastelle (*Barbastella barbastellus*), of which only five colonies were found in a national survey in 2001. If you are in Ebernoe as the light fades on a summer's evening, you may be lucky enough to see barbastelles, as well as the even rarer Bechstein's bats (*Myotis bechsteinii*) emerge. For the first hour or two they will forage under the canopy of the trees until it is dark enough to leave the safety of the woodland, avoid the sparrowhawks and venture farther afield.

Bats are highly protected in Britain and you meddle with their habitat at your peril. Only in very recent years has the Sussex Wildlife Trust been permitted to start restoring the open glades where the cattle grazed – hence the name Ebernoe Common. In most parts of Britain, grazing on common land petered out soon after World War II and, where woodland surrounded the glades that the cattle browsed, trees slowly encroached and shaded out the grasses and wild flowers. At Ebernoe the proof lies in the ancient meadow anthills that you will still find in the undergrowth or beneath the brambles of what has become forest. Now the sunny glades are returning to something like their old splendour as the ever-encroaching scrub is pushed back, step by step, to the feet of the woodland giants. Depending on the time of year you can, as a result, find wild daffodils, bluebells, cowslips, common spotted orchids, ragged robin, devil's-bit scabious, betony and pepper saxifrage scattered here and there. You might also spot sneezewort, an important species that is nationally in decline. Best of all, if you know where to look, you might be rewarded with a treat – a cluster of greater butterfly orchids.

Not that this is all you can see and enjoy. Ebernoe boasts towering beech trees and ancient oaks, and growing beneath many of them is a plant that looks a little like a small holly bush until you get closer. Butchers broom (*Ruscus aculeatus*) has rigid, dark green leaves, sharp and almost diamond shaped. Years ago, sprigs of it were used by butchers to scour the wooden platters on which they displayed and carved their meats. It flourishes only in undisturbed woodlands and, if history and old maps had not already told us that Ebernoe was ancient woodland, the presence of butchers broom would be a powerful clue. So too would be the anthill mounds that you may stumble on as you walk among the glades, for some of these may be as much as 200 years old.

Do not be surprised if, as you wander through the trees, you find yourself being inspected by a small group of Sussex cattle or British whites. The Wildlife Trust brings them in at strategic times of year to browse on any tree or shrub shoots that are threatening to advance into the glades, thus re-establishing the pattern of days gone by that kept the glades open as havens for flowers and insects and, in turn, helped seed- and insect-eating birds to flourish. Woodcock live in these woods and although they are more nocturnal than diurnal, it is worth keeping one's eyes open to see their low, barrelling, zig-zagging flight through the trees if they are disturbed.

In Ebernoe you feel as though you are cradled in the deepest heart of Sussex and yet the border with the most rural and (relatively) empty part of Surrey is just over 2 miles (3 km) to the north as the crow flies. Surrey's Fisherlane and Dunsfold Woods stretch southward into Sussex, linking seamlessly with Kingspark Wood and Birchfield Copse and thence, by way of rews and smaller copses, unbroken woodland rolls onward until it stops at the open fields of Butcherland Farm. Many small mammals and insects, and some wood-dwelling birds, like to move or migrate under cover, and to them the fields of Butcherland

Farm create a barrier over half a mile (1 km) wide between Ebernoe and the continuous woodlands to the north east.

In 2002, the Sussex Wildlife Trust bought these fields with the aim of allowing them to re-afforest naturally. Should you be on the fringes of Ebernoe Common in the autumn you may see the squirrels and jays doing their best to hurry the process along. Ignoring the ever-present buzzards wheeling slowly above the trees, the jays cram as many acorns into their beaks as they can carry, usually three or four at a time, and fly into the fields to bury them for winter use. Scientific observation has shown that they use small shoots or individual tufts of grass as navigational aids to their secret caches, and both squirrels and jays have remarkable memories for what they have buried and where it is. For reasons of security they will even return half way through the season, dig up their remaining caches and rebury them elsewhere. But death in a harsh winter, or faulty calculation, usually means that once summer returns and fresh food is back on the agenda there will be some unused acorns of the 'Sussex weed' ready to germinate. It may take 50 years or longer, but where now a youngster may pause and look northwards across rolling fields he will in old age return to find himself in the middle of a woodland, rich with life, stretching for 4 miles (6 km) or more to north and south of him.

Getting there   National grid ref. SU976278

⊙ Take the A283 Petworth to Haslemere ; pass roundabout with A272, turn right following the direction to Ball's Cross; at Ball's Cross, turn left, pass Butcherland Farm, after half a mile (1 km) turn left, then left again at track signed Ebernoe Church.

Seasonal highlights

◄ *Spring*: nightingales; adders; wild daffodils, bluebells, cowslip, early purple orchids.

◄ *Summer*: butterflies (especially silver-washed fritillary, white admiral, wood white, purple hairstreak, purple emperor); bats; dormice and grass snakes; wild flowers and adder's tongue fern.

◄ *Autumn*: woodcock; lichens (126 of them, making Ebernoe an outstanding national site); mushrooms and fungi (almost 1000 different varieties).

◄ *Winter*: birds (greater spotted woodpeckers, great and long-tailed tits, siskins, goldcrests); lichens and fungi; the structure of the great trees, bare of their leaves.

BURTON POND

WETLAND, WOODLAND & HEATHLAND

The beauties of Burton Pond are many but its greatest appeal is as a collection of habitats all in the same place. Side by side are wetland, woodland and heathland. There are two bogs (one with a boardwalk across it) and, despite the name of the reserve, two lakes, Chingford Pond lying south-west of Burton. The latter was a hammer pond, created in the 16th century by damming streams flowing towards the Rother in order to power giant hammers that crushed rocks for the extraction of iron ore.

If you cross the lane alongside the car park, a well-signed path leads you on a 3-mile (5-km) round walk, starting to the right of the lake. It quickly offers you a diversionary loop to the left, giving a vista across Burton Pond and a chance to glimpse some of the birds that love these conditions, notably great crested grebe, kingfishers, water rail, reed warblers and tufted duck. In summer, water-lilies decorate the surface and in all seasons the fringes are deeply clothed with reeds. On the land-ward side, willow and alder carr keep their feet firmly rooted in the wet soil, but need careful management. Their objective is to march outward into the pond but, if they succeed, they will steadily dry it out, and the reeds will disappear along with the birds that nest in them. Although the shyest of all water birds, the bittern, does not breed here, the male's booming call has been heard on rare occasions, suggesting its willingness to test the water, as it were, for females before flying on.

There is another inhabitant of the reeds, unmoving, unknown else-where in Sussex – and deadly. Cowbane is a member of the carrot family and whilst this makes it sound commonplace it is extremely toxic. The lesser spotted woodpecker, on the other hand, is neither deadly nor as rare but, unlike its cousin the greater spotted, it has an aversion to publicity that means you need to be lucky, keenly observant and in the right place to see it. This is the right place because it is an opportunist that loves the insects found on the edges of woodlands and among the damp, shady alders edging the pond. It is a small, shy bird, no bigger than a sparrow, that likes to keep under cover of the leaves in the tops of the trees. Your best chance of a sighting may be springtime when you might glimpse the male making a mating display flight with its distinctive black and white bars across the wings and back (but without the prominent white shoulder patches of its greater cousin).

When you rejoin the main track you find yourself with different habitats to either side. On the left, below path level, is a small area of wet heath, pink with the flowers of cross-leaved heath in season, where cranberry and sphagnum moss are to be found. On the right are acidic, sandy slopes supporting dry woodland with oak, birch, rowan, sweet chestnut – and badgers. You do not have to look far up the slopes to see large setts that are home to colonies of these endearing (whatever west country dairy farmers may say) but nocturnal animals.

As you walk you may notice that the path once had a man-made surface, though it is now much broken. If you were to explore beneath the growth invading from either side, you would discover that orig-inally it was much wider than it is today. The great house of Burton Park is west of the reserve and, when it was in private ownership, this was one of the two carriageways that led to it. You will come to iron gateposts on either side of the path and the remains of a rusting, decay-ing sign warning visitors to contact the house for the gate to be opened (it was once an electrically operated gate). Once through the gateposts, you will soon have the first of Burton's two bogs, Snipe Bog, on your left, the margins containing clumps of tussock sedge, some of which are over two metres high and three centuries old. Being delicate, the life of the bog is best admired from a distance rather than walked over, and in any case in June you will want to hurry on to see its greatest attraction from a better angle. Turning left onto a metalled lane you will see a wet meadow full of southern marsh orchids. These are counted annually, and in a good year there are as many as 500 but orchids, like most wild flowers, have good, poor and average years. Don't be disappointed, therefore, if sod's law dictates that you have picked a less prolific year!

The path takes you back into woodland and past the north-west end of Chingford Pond where, as dusk falls, large numbers of Daubenton's and pipistrelle bats sometimes skim the surface on their hunting runs and roe deer emerge from the trees to drink at the water's edge. Unlike Burton Pond, Chingford was dug in the mid-18th century as an amenity adding to the attractions of Burton Park House, and the path you follow crosses a Victorian dam that formed a cascade letting the water tumble into the old hammerpond. The channel into which the water fell has now silted up and become a reedbed. Just as alder and willow have to be managed to stop them drying out at Burton Pond, so too the reeds need to be cut by rotation to prevent the open water ultimately becoming a swamp... which brings us seamlessly to the black bog, properly called the Black Hole!

You reach it after following a semi-circular sweep of the path with the fields of the Barlavington estate on one side and, on the other, the water of Burton Pond. By 2002 the Black Hole was choked with alder, birch and willow and in danger of drying out completely, but in that year winches were moved in and the trees were dragged out by the roots. Almost at once, the holes that were left filled with black, peaty water, frogs moved in and in what seemed like no time the surface was covered with frogspawn. The following year the plants that flourish in bogs were returning to their erstwhile glory, and the dragonflies were once more sweeping the water. Yet only five years later birch scrub is plainly visible, leaving no doubt that one day the whole process will have to be repeated if the Black Hole is to continue to play its ecologically important role.

Until that day, the soft mounds of sphagnum moss and the thick mounds of tussock sedge, with hemlock water dropwort, yellow loose-strife and cranberry growing between them, are there to be admired. But the jewels in the crown, as it were, are two delicate beauties – marsh cinquefoil, with its groups of five leaves and its five-pointed crimson flower; and the pretty little bog bean, whose pink-flecked buds open in late May to reveal brilliant white, six-pointed flowers, each petal covered with fluffy white hairs. There are several places at Burton to see some of the 23 species of dragonfly but this is probably the best. Here you can see golden-ringed, black-tailed skimmer, downy emerald, emperor and scarce chaser dragonflies and, perhaps best of the lot, the broad-bodied chaser (*Libellula depressa*) which, as the name implies, has a flatter, broader body than most of its kind. Any time from mid-May to the end of August you may spot them, especially the colourful males with pale blue abdomens and yellow spots on their flanks.

After the Black Hole the slope ahead offers yet another change of habitat. Now you are on dry, acid grassland where lizards and adders love to sun themselves – if only you would let them sleep in peace and stop sending them scurrying for cover! What you will see are the large rounded domes where wood ants live and, since rabbits browse here leaving plentiful droppings behind them, dung beetles at work rolling the pellets towards their little burrows. The other name for dung beetle is scarab, an insect worshipped by the ancient Egyptians with good reason. There are around a thousand kinds of them, beavering away to remove the faeces of animals that would otherwise make the world a smelly, messy place!

Getting there   National grid ref. SU979180
◉ East off the A285 about 2 miles (3 km) south of Petworth.

Seasonal highlights
◅ **Spring**: *water birds; bog and wet woodland flowers.*
◅ **Summer**: *southern marsh orchids; cowbane; dragonflies; water birds.*
◅ **Autumn**: *water birds; hobbies; fungi.*
◅ **Winter**: *redpolls, long-tailed tits, finches; tufted duck, red-headed pochards.*

THE MENS

A FOREST WILDERNESS

Two tips before you set out for The Mens. First, to misquote Dylan Thomas, do not go ill-shod into that dark mud. Except in the driest of summers the paths are splendidly squelchy in many places and wellies or stout walking-boots are *de rigueur*. Secondly, be sure to arm yourself with a compass and before you leave the car park note the direction you will need to get back. The Mens is an untamed forest running approximately north-north-east to south-south-west. Magnificent, awe-inspiring, beautiful — call it what you will — but it is wild and, whilst there are occasional directional arrows on the main path and finger posts at the main junctions, it is easy to lose a sense of direction if you stray off the main track.

The unusual name comes from the Anglo-Saxon *ge mænnes* which, roughly translated, means 'common pasture tenancy', both the name and the size of the forest suggesting that it was common land serving the needs of several parishes. In the 16th and early 17th centuries Kirdford, 2 miles (3 km) to the north, was a major glass-making centre using beech wood in the furnaces, and as this industry fell into decline it was briefly succeeded by iron smelting. These activities did not threaten the commoners' right to pasture and the glades remained open. Converting threat to reality was left to the Mitford family, timber-merchants who acquired Bedham Manor in 1753 and promptly obtained legal rights to enclose large parts of the forest. Although a court case in 1882 rescinded these rights, the glades had almost closed and the forest's character changed, with the result that there are now few trees older than 200 years, except near the northern tip of the reserve where a stand of greater age includes the Idehurst Oak, a sessile oak with a girth of 252 inches (6.4 m). Since 1882 management of the woodland has been sporadic – which is why it is a wilderness, requiring a compass for guidance.

The small car park on lightly-used Crimbourne Lane stands roughly in the middle of the reserve. A footpath on the opposite side of the lane leads towards Idehurst and the ancient sessile oaks, distinguished from the pendunculate oaks normally associated with the south-east of England by their straighter trunks and greater height. Except where it drops briefly to cross a stream the ground to the north of the car park is flat, and most people find the undulating topography of the southern half of the forest more to their taste. In this direction you traverse a steep valley and climb to the heights of Bedham escarpment at the southerly tip, crossing en route the Badlands meadows, full of wild flowers in summer.

Through luck rather more than intent The Mens has been left, almost unmanaged, for over 120 years and this has allowed it to recover naturally from its 18th- and 19th-century depredations. As trees die and fall, or are blown down, they are left. Consequently, fallen branches and trunks are everywhere, some moss-green and writhing like overfed boa constrictors. Because of these arboreal deaths small glades have opened here and there, allowing ground-loving plants to take full advantage of the light before the new-born saplings mature to renew the canopy above. As a result there is a great variety of woodland plants here, from bluebells and wood anemone to wood spurge, broad-leaved helleborine and the delightfully named, though far from uncommon, enchanter's nightshade. In days gone by, marsh violet was even to be seen. There are other advantages resulting from the cycle of growth and decay. The broken limbs of trees provide perfect accommodation for different kinds of bat; woodland butterflies, such as the purple emperor, white admiral and silver-washed fritillary, flutter in the glades; and fallen wood is perfect for fungal growth. This reserve is rich in fungi, the recycling engines of the woods, rotting down organic material. The Mens boasts 483 different species, some of them rare, including three variations of the *Russula* toadstool that are found nowhere else in England.

As you go deeper into the forest the aspect becomes rather more open, with towering beech and oak trees dominant as you drop steadily to the floor of the valley. Beech and oak are not the only inhabitants, however. Infrequently among the 40 or more kinds of tree, wild service is found, with its creamy flowers in May and June, its vivid red autumnal leaves and bark that peels off in rectangular patches, giving it the popular name of chequers tree. In the valley bottom a wide stream cuts a serpentine path through the clay, its sheer sides testimony to the power of water. High and dry on the banks are two small moss- and fern-covered 'dams' marking an earlier generation's failed attempt to control the stream, which simply cut its way round them to form a new channel. In places where sufficient light is available, herb robert, red campion, enchanter's nightshade, wild rose and honeysuckle brighten the summertime banks, and you may spot an occasional warbler flicking its tail as it perches close to the ground. Although the forest is not especially rich in bird life, the insects being too few for all but specialist woodland species, woodcock and the three British woodpeckers (green, greater spotted and lesser spotted) breed here.

After following the stream for a while the path crosses a metalled track and becomes less pronounced until it reaches a narrow plank bridge and a finger post giving a choice of left- or right-hand path. Take the right-hand path and cross the stream because, after a short scramble up a bank, you will emerge into the medieval pasture meadows that are called, misleadingly, Badlands. You enter at the north-east corner through dense bracken and emerge into a different world. Gone is the shaded silence of the great trees, to be replaced, in summertime, by the hum of bees, butterflies browsing for nectar, crickets and grasshoppers everywhere and a gently waving mosaic of yellow, red and purple. Britain has lost 95 per cent of its unimproved grasslands, and these two fields remind us of what we have sacrificed – knapweed, agrimony, betony, red clover, devil's bit scabious, St John's wort, tormentil, dyer's greenweed and bird's foot trefoil (not to mention the cowslips and primulas of spring) will make you linger. And there are greater delicacies to be looked for – lady's mantle, adder's tongue ferns, greater butterfly orchids and maybe, just maybe, the rare lesser butter-fly orchid (*Platanthera bifolia*).

When you are ready to return to the majesty of the forest, look for a pedestrian gate on the south-east flank of the furthest field. The way (signed) jinks round a picturesque smallholder's cottage and barn, a reminder that 23 households still have commoners' rights in The Mens. After a little while you come to a crossroads with finger posts. If you take the right-hand path you begin a long but rewarding haul up the escarpment to Bedham on its ridge. This is perfect beech forest, dark and thickly clustered at first, with an undergrowth of holly, but gradually thinning out to display a brown carpet of fallen leaves, with here and there bumps and hollows of past workings or the outline of earthen banks marking ancient boundaries. At any moment you may glimpse a deer – fallow possibly, roe certainly and the shyest of all, the little muntjac. It is impossible to resist the urge to rest and drink in the cathedral of soaring trunks and the silence that would be absolute but for the background murmuring of pigeons. Should a gust of wind disturb the leaves above, the sound is almost shocking.

Eventually you emerge onto Wakestone Lane at the south-east corner of the reserve. If you still have the energy, turn right for a few hundred yards and, just below the level of the road, you will be looking down into a curiosity, a roofless, abandoned chapel in what seems like the remotest spot for miles. If not, get out your compass and start on back to the main car park!

Getting there   National grid ref. TQ023236
❿ A272, 2 miles (3 km) west of Wisborough Green, turn left to Crimbourne.

Seasonal highlights

◀ *Spring: springtime flowers; woodpeckers on mating flights.*
◀ *Summer: Badlands wild flowers; magnificent stands of beech and oak.*
◀ *Autumn: fungi and lichens; Badlands autumn flowers.*
◀ *Winter: the haunting solitude of a leafless wilderness; Herdwick sheep grazing the Badlands.*

PULBOROUGH BROOKS

BIRDS & SOME BATS

Because the greater part of Pulborough Brooks is a flood plain it would be too easy – and very wrong – to assume it is flat, boring, wet and of interest only to those who get a kick out of herons and ducks. While not denying the presence of water it is, on the contrary, a charming spot, with beautiful views to the South Downs across the wet grasslands of the Arun valley. There are high meadows and hedgerows, copses and rews to provide habitat for birds of woodland and meadow as well as those of water. In addition, there are primroses and bluebells to gladden the eye in spring, purple loosestrife and flag irises in the ditches and a rich variety of other wildlife. But, given that this is one of the flagship reserves of the Royal Society for the Protection of Birds (RSPB), birds are the inevitable stars of the show, even if you are just as likely to look out from a hide and see a fallow deer grazing 30 yards (30 m) away or, almost in front of you, a grey squirrel holding a mushroom in its paws, and chomping on it contentedly.

The reserve is open all year between 9 am and 5 pm (with a side entrance from which you can let yourself out after hours if you are owl watching). There is an entry charge, currently £3.50, for non-members of the RSPB and what you get in return is an excellently maintained site with firm footpaths, clear signposting, plenty of benches and perches from which to stop and observe, four hides looking over different areas of the reserve and a series of interesting information boards about the lifestyle of the many different kinds of birds to be seen. There is also a modern visitor centre and café, with a bird-feeding area in front of it where chaffinches, greenfinches, nuthatches and tits may well be pre-occupied, and an area where children can watch and learn. Binoculars are available for hire.

The visitor centre stands on the high ground, the reserve sloping away from it. It is the starting point of a circular trail, 2 miles (3 km) long, with high pasture fields at its core and flood meadows, ponds and drainage ditches on the outside of the loop. Much of the way you pass through scattered copses and rews, with little glades here and there in which, in high summer, dragonfly and butterfly activity may be more apparent than that of birds. Among the latter, common blues, holly blues, brown argus and small coppers are likely to be here in numbers on a warm day.

The first and largest of the meadows round which the trail leads is described as a gigantic bird table for the summer feeders – seed-eaters such as linnets, yellowhammers, reed buntings and goldfinches, and insect hunters like lapwings, thrushes and skylarks. The RSPB maintains an 'old-fashioned' approach to farming its high meadows. Until the 1960s most crops in Britain were sown in spring, which meant that, when the field was mown in autumn, there was abundant stubble in which insects and fallen seeds were plentiful, providing vital winter food for wintering birds. Nowadays, the majority of crops are winter sown and so, for example, skylark numbers are in steady decline. This endearing little bird that is liable to flutter straight up into the air from almost beneath your feet, singing lustily, used to produce two or three broods in a year in the old, spring-sowing, days. With winter sowing it manages only one.

The hedgerows and scrub along the margins of the fields harbour insects and small mammals, perfect hunting territory for bats and owls once dusk has fallen. Among the six species of bat here are noctules, natterers and long-eared bats, the last of these being particularly interesting because studies have shown that, unlike most bats, the brown long-eared prefers to track its insect prey using visual rather than echo-location methods. Being a bat where barn owls are present can be a hazardous business, because although mice, voles, shrews and small rats are the owls' staple diet, some are not above taking other hedgerow hunters, such as finches or bats, given the chance. Barn owls nest at Pulborough Brooks, and in some springs a camera in their roost enables you to watch the chicks on a screen in the visitor centre. Except in spring, when there are chicks to feed, you are unlikely to see a barn owl out and about during the day whereas the semi-diurnal short-eared owl might well be seen after dawn or before dusk surveying its hunting area whilst perched on a stump, in a tree or even on the ground.

There is one inhabitant of the hedgerows that is especially close to people's hearts – and ears – the nightingale. Among the highlights of the year is the period from April to early June when nightingales are in full song both by day and night. They nest in thick hedges, scrub or the edges of woodland, often with water nearby, and are as difficult to spot as they are easy on the ear. The southern half of England is the limit of their range and Sussex, with its greater share of woodland, one of its fastnesses. Even so, national numbers have declined by almost half in the last three decades, and there are thought to be only between 5000 and 6000 of this migrant bird still visiting in spring and summer. So if you want to enjoy the marvellous melodies and variations of this harmonious songster whilst you may, this is the place to come.

The four hides around the nature trail face north, west and south but all look out over ponds and flood meadows or, to give them a more formal name, lowland wet grasslands, a rapidly diminishing habitat in Britain thanks to pollution, poor management and the growing demand for water made by drier winters and increasing population. In the spring, lapwing, redshank and snipe nest among the long, tussocky grass, snipe in nests built by the male, and lapwing and redshank in scrapes. All three are long-legged waders that probe the soft ground for earthworms and hunt for invertebrates such as spiders and damselfly larvae. The lapwing (or peewit, because of its call) is probably the most distinctive of the three, partly because of the long crest that flicks upward from the back of the head, and partly because, in autumn and winter, large flocks can be seen in lazy flight or settling on a high pasture to forage for insects.

Another bird to watch for from March onwards is a rare summer visitor that arrives from Iberia and southern France – the yellow wagtail. This is a bird that is in danger of being moved from amber to red on the list of endangered species as land is drained for agriculture, which makes all the more welcome its appearance at the tail of the cattle brought in to graze the flood meadows in summer. Newly hatched yellow wagtails do not leave their parents after fledging but stay with the family unit, following the cattle to feed on the flies and beetles that gather round their dung.

It would be impossible to leave the ponds without mentioning the wintertime flocks of ducks and waders. Some are here virtually through-out the year – shelduck, gadwall, shoveler, mallard, coot and moorhen, for example – but the arrival of migrating wigeon, teal and pintail on the flooded meadows is worth waiting for. It is thought that more than 25,000 pintails fly in from Russia and Finland to winter in England, but their numbers are in serious decline and no more than 40 pairs are reckoned to breed in this country, so it is worth being on the lookout for the male's long black tail that gives the species its name. And it is also worth looking out for something spectacular but more sobering. The winter flocks attract the birds of prey, sparrowhawks, hen harriers and peregrines, and it is quite something to watch a harrier sweeping across its territory. If you are lucky enough to be in the right place at the right time, the sight of a peregrine stooping at over 100 miles an hour (160 kph) to take a duck on the wing is a spectacle likely to disappoint only the victim!

Getting there National grid ref. TQ058164
◑ Off the west side of the A283 Pulborough-Storrington road.

Seasonal highlights
◄ *Spring: nightingales; spring flowers; adders and grass snakes.*
◄ *Summer: owls and nightjars at dusk; butterflies; dragonflies.*
◄ *Autumn: redstarts and whinchats; arrival of the first winter ducks; fungi.*
◄ *Winter: flocks of ducks and waders; birds of prey; fieldfares and redwing.*

NYMANS WOODS

TALL TREES & SANDSTONE ROCKS

Cow Wood, Brickyard Wood, Tanyard Wood, Stonepit Wood, Marl Pit Shaw, Furnace Green... these names, evocative of the uses to which this classic High Weald woodland was once put, today coalesce into the all-embracing name of Nymans Woods. Unless you are a member of the National Trust, with access to the ruined house and famous gardens below which the woods lie, you can take a direct public path into them from the village sign at the southern end of Handcross High Street. This leads you down to a crossroads. Keep straight on and the adventure begins. The path plunges down like the track of a big dipper towards the depths of Cow Wood Ghyll and in places as it does so there are earthen banks on either side. These mark the passage of thousands of journeys on foot by earlier generations of villagers making their daily way to noisy, smelly work in the furnace, the tanyard, the stone or the marl pits.

Once you reach the bottom you have a choice: in April you can bear right on an upward path that will take you through the beeches and round past a prolific display of bluebells, turning the slopes a vivid blue beneath the budding trees; or you can take the path along the floor of the ghyll. The headwaters of the river Ouse are close by, and the route follows the moss covered banks of a small stream murmuring down towards a lake that was a hammer pond in the days when the woods rang with the noise of industry. Like Eridge Rocks (*see p.64*) these woods also were once choked with *Rhododendron ponticum*, quelling all competition from other plants with their lethal habits. It redoubles the sense of wonder that where there were impenetrable masses of rhododendron and, before that, the din and bustle of work, there is now such peace beneath the cool canopy of great beeches.

Whichever route you take you will arrive at a point where the paths meet again and two things will strike you: sandstone rocks reminiscent, on a smaller scale, of those at Eridge Rocks; and a very tall tree, the tallest in Sussex to be exact, which was 160 feet (48.5 m) high when last measured in April 2007. It is a Wellingtonia, one of a series of Californian redwoods (*Sequoiadendron giganteum*) and grand firs, planted as an avenue in 1910, by which time the woods were long since in use as an amenity for Nymans, the big house above. These great trees love the moist, cool conditions close to the stream, but the redwoods may come to pose an interesting problem some time in the second half of the 21st century for two reasons. First, they coppice easily, so if one falls it will readily sprout fresh shoots from the bottom, thus replacing one with many. Secondly, although redwoods can set seed when they are little more than grouchy arboreal teenagers, they are very long-lived trees and approach maximum fertility between the ages of 150 and 200. As the existing trees are approaching their hundredth birthdays it means major changes might be taking place here in the second half of the 21st century. If you bring your children on a walk here, you could suggest they come back as old men or women to check if there are rings of baby redwoods where now there are only giants!

The rocks are a clue to why Cow Wood Ghyll is called by the West Sussex name of ghyll (and in Yorkshire and East Sussex, gill), rather than valley. Strictly speaking a ghyll has rocks on either side with a fault between them from which the clay filling has been washed out by erosion. One rock here stands out, literally and figuratively, from the others – Pulpit Rock. The name is said to come from its use by a clergyman named Pook as a pulpit from which to preach to the workers in the woods. The wood rising behind it, where the concentration of bluebells is greatest, is called Pookchurch Wood in his honour.

The lake was substantially widened in the 19th century – another change wrought for pleasure by the inhabitants of the big house – and gudgeon, stickleback and eels are at home in it, as are crested newts. Water-loving trees like alder and willow grow around it and plants such as greater stitchwort, marsh thistle and water iris find the conditions to their liking. Most eye-catching of all for many people are the dragonflies and damselflies found here, along the streams and over both the shady and the sunny pools scattered through the woods. Fourteen species have been recorded, among them the brilliant emerald dragonfly (*Somatochlora metallica*), which is common in Sussex and Kent but is scarce elsewhere in the country. Two of the most attractive species are usually plentiful – the golden ringed dragonfly and the beautiful demoiselle damselfly with its metallic, bluish-green body and bluish brown wings – and both are happiest around fast-flowing streams. The other uncommon variety here is the white legged damselfly (*Platycnemis pennipes*). This can be found on more sluggish streams or rivers, but it is worth being alert for its distinctive broad, feathery, white legs and (in the males) striking pale blue body with an occasional black hoop.

At the lake you have a choice of paths, to the left or right. Either will bring you in contact with one of the two meadows in the woods, Furnace Green and Keeper's Field. Both have lain fallow for years but, by a pattern of regular cutting and grazing, the National Trust intends to restore them to the wild flower rich meadows that would have been common when cattle were pastured in them. When the objective is achieved, the birds and butterflies will not be slow to take advantage although there are already many in the glades, where species like early purple and common spotted orchids, and the rare ivy leaf bellflower, blossoming in June and July, can be found. There are 47 varieties of bird breeding here and among the butterflies are large and small skippers, silver washed and high brown fritillaries, purple emperors, white admirals, peacocks and commas.

Whichever way you turn at the lake will lead you towards colourful displays of flowers in the spring. If you go left, you will happen upon celandines, primroses, ladies smock and wood anemones. If you turn right and climb through Furnace Green you will come to an ancient track, worn down to its present level by generations going to the iron workings, and on the banks above are primroses, bluebells and, in particular, wild daffodils, smaller, more delicate and more beautiful than the cultivated varieties that brighten our gardens. If you remain on this path it will eventually turn and drop down into Foxhole Ghyll below another line of sandstone cliffs that harbour rare mosses and ferns.

The great storm of October 1987 destroyed five million trees in Sussex and wrought havoc in this ghyll. A few Douglas firs survived but the far greater numbers of casualties were replaced in 1991 by a planting of oaks. In the bottom of the ghyll are a series of cascade pools, built after World War I, and the reason why you may be lucky enough to spot not only dragonflies but the flash of a kingfisher at work. In the spring your nostrils may be assailed by the unpleasant smell of the aptly named skunk cabbages as they throw up their yellow flowers. These aliens escaped from gardens by being washed downstream and may have to be controlled one day. In the meantime they are spectacular plants even when the flowers have gone and the aroma abated and as they serve to bring a faintly tropical feeling to the ghyll, enjoy them while you can!

For the most unusual plant of all you must hunt in March in Nightingale Woods, west of the house and gardens on the other side of the B2114 road. Toothwort (*Lathraea squamaria*) contains no chlorophyll and therefore no green colouring. It is a parasitic plant that pushes a pinkish spike through the ground, hung with white tooth-like flowers (hence the name). Its attraction is rarity rather than beauty, but if you spot it among the dead leaves of early spring you will deserve further bragging rights and a pat on the back.

Getting there   National grid ref. TQ263294
◗ Off the A23 at Handcross, south of Crawley.

Seasonal highlights
◀ *Spring*: woodland flowers.
◀ *Summer*: dragonflies and damselflies; butterflies.
◀ *Autumn*: mosses and ferns.
◀ *Winter*: the sandstone rocks; the streams, pools and cascades.

BEDELANDS FARM

WILD FLOWER MEADOWS

In 1994 it was estimated that only 10,000 acres (4000 hectares) of species-rich neutral grassland remained in Britain. To you and me this means wild flower meadows, so it is a relief to say we have some in Sussex and few, if any, are likely to be better than those within the Bedelands Farm Nature Reserve. Don't be put off by the unpromising beginning in the concrete car park adjoining the local football clubs' pitches. Take the path round the end of them and prepare to enter a different – and altogether charming – world via Leylands Wood and Long Wood, two strips of woodland at the bottom of what might be thought of as a 100 acre (40 hectare) oval.

At the top of the oval is lily-covered Valebridge Pond. Below it to the west is ancient Big Wood, and to the east is Valebridge Common. Enclosed between the woods to the north, west and south is a system of meadows bearing the evocative names of Watford Meadow, Wet Meadow, Big (because it is) Field and Old Arable. About seven centuries ago these fields were cleared out of the forest that once stretched southwards from here to the foot of the South Downs in order to create farmland, whereas the fields of Valebridge Common have been open common land for more than a millennium, and were once clothed in gorse and bracken.

If you start your visit by taking the path westward through Leyland Wood you will come to Watford Meadow at the south-west corner of the reserve and just before you enter the field there is the curiosity of a large tree stump, some 10 feet (3 m) tall, with shoulders broader than its foot. This is an ancient hornbeam, hollow yet still putting out shoots and attempting to grow. It is a reminder that in bygone days our ancestors used trees, or made earthen banks, to mark the edges of their territories. The reason this large stump is broad-shouldered is clear enough if you look closely – at some stage in its life it was pollarded, probably on a regular cycle. When you get to Big Wood in the north of the reserve, you will find some magnificent examples of coppiced hornbeams whose stools have grown to a great size.

But first, take a stroll through the fields. Watford is a typical wealden meadow, and in late spring and early summer ladies smock, yellow rattle, red clover and common spotted orchids are abundant here. Big Field was once two fields with a hedge arcing in a rough semi-circle across it. If you come in late April you will see its former path picked out by the bluebells that began life in its shadow. If hedges that have been undisturbed for generations are your thing, then make for the one that forms the western boundary of Big Field. It provides magnificent cover for a wealth of insects and small mammals, and a nesting site for birds.

A boardwalk runs up the western edge of Wet Meadow and if, in a dry summer, you are tempted to wonder why it has such a name, look for the rushes growing here and the tell-tale dips in the ground that are bare of growth. Alternatively, come back in winter to find out! The whole site sits on wealden clay, after all, and no locals need any reminder to put their wellies on in wet weather. Come spring and early summer, though, and apart from the bugle and all three kinds of buttercup growing here you will be enchanted by the drifts of the less common ragged robin that splash the grass with red.

Since the Mid-Sussex District Council acquired Bedelands in 1991, the University of Sussex has played a major role in helping to restore its meadows. This is being achieved mainly through a careful programme of cutting at strategic times of year, followed by sheep grazing. This keeps the grasses down and reduces the thatch produced by them at ground level, allowing wild flowers to germinate and spread naturally. As you stroll through the meadows, therefore, you may come across areas fenced off (currently this is to be found in Old Arable) so that the University can monitor the results of the grazing programme at different times of the year.

From Old Arable your footsteps will inevitably lead you into Big Wood, most ancient of all the woodland areas here. There are several ponds that are home to yellow flags, branched burr-weed and, in some of them, tussock sedge, a plant to be found in the Black Bog at Burton Pond (see p.32) but rarely elsewhere. And where there is water and vegetation there are likely to be dragonflies and damselflies to delight the eye, flashing and wheeling over the surface.

Big Wood has springtime carpets of wood anemones and bluebells and a magnificent mix of trees. Massive hornbeam, many coppiced, are dominant but here are plentiful oaks, birch, wild service, field maple and wild cherry trees, each fighting to get its head above the canopy and take the major share of light. A superb specimen of wild service stands on the eastern edge of the wood and about 100 yards (90 m) to the north is an equally fine example, but this one is coppiced. Both are close to the prominent bank and ditch that for something like 1200 years has marked the boundary between the lord of the manor's land (the wood) and Valebridge common. As you follow the path northward along the line of this ancient division the sound of rushing water gradually interrupts your thoughts. A short path to your right takes you out of the wood and round to two narrow wooden bridges over the dam that forms Valebridge Pond. In June, it is spectacular with yellow brandy bottle water lilies covering the surface.

Now, as you turn southwards to start wandering back, it is time to luxuriate in the opulence of Valebridge Common. This is grassland so rich in species that you feel the grass itself is the one that struggles to make its presence felt! Here you will find bulbous buttercup — less often encountered than creeping or meadow buttercup; you will also see, in season, black knapweed, self heal, tufted vetch and the enchanting grass vetchling with its handsome crimson flowers; there are common spotted orchids and adder's tongue fern in abundance. But the crowning glory is everywhere in this meadow – dyers greenweed (*Genista tinctoria*).

Dyer's greenweed! I can almost hear cries of 'what an anticlimax!' and indeed it isn't much of a name, so given because it was once used to make dyes. But it is a beauty, it is very rare and it enjoys abundance in this meadow that may not be equalled anywhere else. In May its light green stems are already 6 to 9 inches (15 to 23 cm) tall; between mid-June and early July it has attained its full 12 inches (28 cm) and is ready to burst out in spires of copious yellow, ear-shaped flowers reminiscent of those on broom, with which it shares the Latin name *Genista*. It is, quite simply, a glory – provided the bug that sometimes attacks it stays away – and the prospect of seeing a large field full of it at the end of June could tempt you to part with money.

It follows that where there are abundant wild flowers there will be hosts of butterflies, and so there are in Bedelands. Gatekeepers and meadow browns are the most frequently seen – in the case of the latter nearly 2000 times in 2006 – but you are also likely to spot ringlet, small copper and common blue, white admiral and red admiral, painted lady, small tortoiseshell, clouded yellow, green hairstreak and marbled white. As for the birds, 60 species were recorded in 2006, including kingfisher, water rail, marsh tit, mistle thrush and, for the first time, lapwing, reed bunting and reed warbler. And it is comforting to know that many birds that were once familiar in our gardens but are now in decline across the country seem to be thriving in Bedelands – song thrush, starling, bullfinch, house sparrow, fieldfare, meadow pipit, goldcrest, redwing and grey wagtail.

Getting there   National grid ref. TQ320208

❯ Take the A273 to Burgess Hill, turn left south of the double roundabout, turn left along Leylands Road, follow signs to Bedelands Farm Nature Reserve.

Seasonal highlights

◀ *Spring & summer: wild flowers and butterflies.*

◀ *Summer & autumn: wild flowers; dragonflies and damselflies; birds.*

◀ *Winter: fungi (e.g. waxcaps); the leafless geometry of ancient trees in Big Wood.*

CHAILEY COMMON

FIVE IN ONE

Chailey Common is more or less the dead centre of Sussex and, to reinforce the sense of centrality, a stone at its north-eastern extremity marks the point where the Greenwich Meridian passes through it, dividing east from west. Despite its unifying name, this local nature reserve is actually five commons, each with its own little car park, straddling the A272 road and bounded on the east by the A275. On its western flank is Romany Ridge Common which, moving east, adjoins Pound and then Memorial Commons. Due north of Memorial lies Red House Common, and to the north east, separated by perhaps half a mile of kms, is the outlying Lane End Common where the Meridian stone stands, erected in 1953.

The name Chailey comes from the Anglo-Saxon words for gorse (chag) and field (leghe). The gorse, head high and more, remains in abundance – providing you can see it (in summer and autumn) for the equally towering bracken. When a rise in the land gives you a view across the common it is like looking out over a sea of green, broken by the occasional lone pine or a stunted oak struggling to achieve the majestic structure that its brothers, firmly rooted in wealden clay, regard as their birthright. But this is acidic lowland heath, a nationally rare habitat of which Sussex boasts more than its national share.

The plants that thrive in these conditions are those that can exist on a sparse diet of nutrients, for the soil is impoverished by centuries of over-use. Generations of peasants exercised their common land rights to cut wood for fuel and bracken for bedding and floor covering, whilst their cattle and sheep were set free to graze the shoots of incipient trees, such as the invasive birch. Since the custom of grazing died away after World War II the bracken and birch have run riot. This is all too evident today, but work to recreate the traditional lowland heath is under way, albeit in its early stages. Swathes of bracken are cut in midsummer and, bit by bit, this weakens its underground root system until, after five years or so, its growth is sufficiently stunted to allow grasses, ling, bell heather and cross-leaved heath the space and light to re-establish them-selves, and the pink and purple of their flowers to colour the common once again. So the message is one of patience. Volunteers and contrac-tors are beavering away and, year by year, they, and you, are rewarded with another step taken towards the restoration of this ancient heath.

The ground at Romany Ridge falls gently away from the car park, offering a classic heathland view across the shallowest of valleys. The broad base of this depression is boggy, full of small peaty pools and tussocky grass. Until recently, mature birch trees dominated the floor of the valley, drying out the bog, and much work has been done to uproot them. The labour of preventing scrub re-infesting the area is now entrusted to a flock of black hebridean sheep, who chew bramble and birch shoots in a quest to create ideal conditions for bog asphodel, marsh gentians and carnivorous sundews, whose sticky tendrils attract insects to their doom. Bog asphodel, with its star-like yellow flowers from July to September, is not a great rarity, whereas the marsh gentian (*Gentiana pneumonanthe*) is a much less common plant of acidic bogs and wet heath. It needs light grazing to reduce the competition from more vigorous contenders, and space to germinate, but its striking, trumpet-shaped purple flower is well worth searching for between the months of July and October.

The four other Commons climb gradually onto higher ground and lack the boggy conditions found at Romany Ridge. Along the way the bright yellow flowers of creeping tormentil, smaller in its heathland than its woodland form, spangle the edges of the broader paths and rides in summer. At the other end on the scale of magnitude, red spires of rosebay willow-herb poke up at every turn. As common as muck it may be and a pest when it invades the garden, but when we are so often fighting to save wild flowers in danger of extinction this is one that bucked the trend. Fireweed is its common name and after showing signs of decline in the 19th century the clearance of ground for timber in World War I, and the bombing of World War II, gave it the chance to stage a comeback.

This, though, is reptile country where common lizards are often to be seen on warm, sunny days, and where adders are comfortably at home. Adders are Britain's only venomous snake, but their toxin is slight and you would have to be very sick or very young to be in danger if bitten – a most unlikely occurrence since they would strike only if backed into an inescapable corner and there are few, if any, of those in the 450 acres of Chailey Common. Indeed, it would be almost as unlikely as witnessing their extraordinary courtship behaviour. Stags lock horns and wrestle, and birds of paradise display to impress a potential mate, but male adders have climbing contests, using themselves as ladders. Two males will coil round each other, one seeking to climb higher than the other to demonstrate its supremacy, until both appear to be balanced on the tips of their tails. It is a sight rarely seen, and one to be savoured.

If, after this, you are in need of peaceful views to soothe the breast, one of the best is from the 1971 monument at the southern end of Memorial Common commemorating the determination of Garth Christian and Charles Constant to preserve this common as a nature reserve. The ground drops sharply, enhancing the fine vista to the ridge of the South Downs and the swell of Ditchling Beacon. In June and early July it is as well to keep your eyes peeled as you walk for the pale pink of the heath spotted orchid. Only slight variations in the lower lip of the flower distinguish this orchid from the common spotted, although the dark blotches on the leaves are usually smaller and more numerous on the heath spotted. But who cares? They are both orchids, equally beautiful, and both give the heart a bounce when you find them. By the time you reach Red House Common you are at the highest point of the reserve. The north-easterly edge of the common falls away to a valley below, opening up views to the north and north-west of the prominent sandstone ridge that, geologically speaking, is so different from the heathland.

Of all the times of the year to enjoy Chailey Common, spring must be the best, not just because the bracken has yet to grow and obscure the sweeping views of heath. Spring is the time when birdsong is everywhere as chaffinches, tits and nuthatches establish their territories before the summer migrants, the warblers, arrive. They give eager and frequent voice to their warnings that here they are and here they intend to stay – not to mention the enthusiasm with which they sing an altogether different song designed for the ears of a prospective mate. Late spring is also the time when the early butterflies are on the wing – yellow brimstones, tortoiseshells and peacocks. By July and August ringlets are everywhere, so named because of the three little rings at the edge of each dark brown leading wing, with another two on each tail wing. On the other hand the uncommon silver-studded blue butterfly, so successful on Stedham Common (*see p.16*) is seen less and less at Chailey. It may be that its recovery awaits the restoration of more extensive drifts of the bell heather on which its caterpillar lives. But if this is one rarity that is struggling here, another – a bird – is thriving. The Dartford warbler is a shy bird that will flutter apologetically into the heart of the densest gorse if you disturb it but, however fleeting the glimpse, at least you have seen a bird thriving that was nearly killed off completely by the freezing winter of 1963.

Getting there   National grid ref. TQ388216
❱ A272, Haywards Heath-Uckfield road and A275, Lewes-Wych Cross;
   the Commons are to the north and west of where the roads cross.

Seasonal highlights
◀ *Spring*: birdsong; early butterflies; open views.
◀ *Summer*: birds (early); lizards and adders; orchids; ling and heather; bog plants.
◀ *Autumn*: birds.
◀ *Winter*: open vistas across the heath.

OLD LODGE

HIGH HEATH IN ASHDOWN FOREST

Old Lodge is a special site in a special area – Ashdown Forest. In any weather, be it mid-summer sunshine or early winter drizzle, the Old Lodge reserve exudes a magic that is undiminished even in the kind of mist in which Pooh and Piglet tried to lose Rabbit in the Hundred Acre Wood. Pooh and his friends would have felt at home at Old Lodge, even though Pooh Country is a mile or so to the north. Ashdown Forest is special because it is the largest heathland in the south east and, in the world as a whole, heathland is rarer than tropical forest. Within this landscape Old Lodge is special for many reasons. It is a managed reserve and, as any expert will tell you, many of the species that heathland supports would vanish without continuous management. It is an area of mixed woodland and heath land, with a greater concentration of small ponds (many created by volunteers) than can be found elsewhere in the Forest, and this allows a greater diversity of species. Old Lodge is also close to the highest part of the Forest and offers splendid views to north and south. There is a point from which you can see Box Hill on the North Downs in one direction and, by turning 180 degrees, Chanctonbury Ring on the South Downs. Yet being bisected by a steep-sided valley the visitor is also rewarded with delightful internal vistas within the heart of the reserve.

There is a small, unsurfaced car park at the eastern tip of the site, and a 2-mile (3-km), circular walk around it, in the course of which you may spot the occasional shallow pit like many others that can be encountered throughout the Forest. These may well be the last vestiges of the days when Sussex, and Ashdown Forest in particular, was the industrial heartland of England. The rocks beneath the surface contain iron ore and Britain's first blast furnace was built in 1496 at Newbridge, near present-day Coleman's Hatch. Massive quantities of charcoal were needed to satisfy the voracious appetites of the furnaces that spread through the area, and what had been a protected hunting forest since 1283 was progressively stripped of its timber for over three hundred years. In his *Rural Rides*, William Cobbett described Ashdown Forest in 1822 as

> *verily the most villainously ugly spot I ever saw in England… instead of trees black, rugged, hideous rocks.*

He would be a happy man if he were to come back today, for now the deer roam freely and the birds trill their mating calls.

If you start the circular walk round Old Lodge by heading northwest you will pass through small, picturesque groups of pine, with gorse and ling crowding together but never overpowering the walker's sense of being on heathland. On this part of the reserve, the gorse grows less high than elsewhere, thanks to what was taken out of the soil by past usage, and it is noticeable that the many patches of springtime bluebells are also closer to the ground than their woodland sisters who have the benefit of rich leaf mould.

As the path turns west it begins to drop down a slope towards a belt of woodland guarded by three magnificent beeches of such perfect size, shape and proportion that, for a moment, you could almost believe a topiarist had been at work with giant shears. May is the perfect month to see these beautiful trees when they are newly clothed with fresh, light green leaves that almost sparkle in the late spring sunshine. As you walk on you will see some of the ponds that have been created here. Insect-eating sundews grow around them and the large raft spider (*Dolomedes fimbriatus*), with its distinctive white stripe down each flank, is at home in their neighbourhood. The raft spider attracts prey, such as damselflies and even small fishes, by vibrating its front legs on the surface of the water. It is the largest spider native to Britain, and the females can grow to nearly an inch long (22 mm). There are 24 species of dragonfly and damselfly to be seen at Old Lodge – golden ringed dragonflies prefer the streams, but keeled skimmers have been seen on nine of the ponds, black darters are colonising here and, perhaps best of all, the rare small red damselfly is avoiding the clutches of the raft spider to good effect. The first pair was seen in 1996, but a decade later as many as 93 were counted in a single day.

The downward slope increases markedly as you drop into a pretty, steep-sided valley. At the right time of year the russet of old bracken provides an attractive foreground to the dark green of pines and the lighter green of deciduous trees climbing the opposite slopes, whilst to the north the hillsides are reminiscent less of the Weald than of northern moors. Ashdown Forest as a whole is home to fallow and roe deer, and even little muntjacs, albeit in small numbers. Old Lodge's habitat is suitable mainly for fallow deer. Over 70 were recently counted in what appeared to be a single herd, so you stand a chance of seeing one of these extraordinarily handsome animals should you happen upon them when you are upwind and their super-sensitive nostrils fail to detect you. The fallow deer generally rut in the second half of October, the males making loud groaning noises as they issue challenges preparatory to jousting for females, and if you encounter them then they are likely to have little time for you as long as you don't get too close.

There are 11 other wild animals at Old Lodge, and as they are part of the management team you are more than likely to encounter them. They are Exmoor ponies, devoting their lives to cropping the grass and enabling wild flowers such as heath bedstraw, heath spotted orchids and petty whin (needle furze) to flourish. Dogs are not encouraged at Old Lodge, although they may be taken on a short lead if you insist, in which case a word of warning is in order. Exmoor ponies are wild. They may well find your dog an animal of almost irresistible curiosity and will crowd around to inspect it at close quarters if given half a chance, something to which it — or the ponies — may react unpredictably.

Right across Ashdown Forest bird life is plentiful with 110 species recorded as residents or visitors, including migrants such as the great grey shrike. But here again Old Lodge is special because of the diversity offered by its heath, pines and deciduous woods. Springtime is the outstanding season when it plays host to favourites like green and greater spotted woodpeckers, stonechats, dunnocks and linnets, with lesser redpoll, chaffinches and great tits flitting among the pines. As spring merges into summer, blackcaps, whitethroats, crossbills, tree pipits and swallows arrive, as do woodcock and nightjars. But the redstarts and woodlarks are given particular devotion at Old Lodge.

Nesting boxes are provided – and regularly monitored – for redstarts, and you may well see them on the wing in early summer catching flying insects. The males, with their black faces, white foreheads and orange breasts, are particularly eye-catching. It is the woodlark that has probably benefited most from the careful management of the reserve. This appealing little bird, with its tufted crest, is a fussy character that knows exactly what it likes. It requires soft soil or bracken peat in which to scrape a nest, preferably in the shadow of heather or grass tussocks, and likes bare ground on which to forage for spiders, caterpillars and beetles during the breeding season. It is also partial to the fringes of woods, ideally scalloped into gentle bays, on which to perch while scanning the ground for food. Old Lodge is one of those places that provides what it needs, and can share in the satisfaction of knowing that the dramatic decline of this bird in Britain, which had fallen to as few as 250 pairs in 1986, has been triumphantly reversed over the last two decades.

Getting there   National grid ref. TQ469306
> About a third of mile (0.5 km) north of the junction of B2026
Hartfield-Maresfield road with B2188 from Groombridge.

Seasonal highlights
* *Spring*: birds.
* *Summer*: birds; dragonflies; lizards and adders; heather in flower.
* *Autumn*: dwarf gorse (late summer flowering); fungi (over 200 species).
* *Winter*: the views, magnificent in any season.

PARK CORNER HEATH

BUTTERFLY HEAVEN

Park Corner Heath is a small reserve, 10 acres (4 hectares), devoted to the happiness and well-being of butterflies in particular and dragonflies, reptiles and birds co-incidentally. At its core is an area of heath, criss-crossed by paths and fringed by woodland, set within an ancient forest; even if your interest in butterflies extends no further than regarding them as reminders of balmy summer days, you will still enjoy an hour's stroll round this tranquil reserve.

The approach to the heath has a grace that would credit a stately home, the broad track being lined on one side by mature beech trees topping an earthen bank that would once have marked a boundary. Passing a pond lined with reeds and bulrushes you enter the open heath where the Sussex Branch of Butterfly Conservation has placed a hut for you to pause and observe and learn more about the butterflies you might see as you walk the reserve. A board has pictures of those known to be present with descriptions of their habits. Almost as helpful is a book in which visitors are invited to record what they have seen. You might read there, for example, that only yesterday three silver-washed fritillaries, six peacocks, eight gatekeepers and multiple meadow browns had been seen. You are instantly alerted to what is likely to be out and about at the time you have chosen to visit, and you find yourself studying the pictures with renewed enthusiasm to be sure you, too, will recognise them if they flutter within your view.

Another thing that emerges from the book is the frequency with which adders, slow worms and common lizards are seen around the heath. The sunnier the day the better the chance that reptiles will be recharging their metabolisms in the warmth, especially in spring and early summer. Here and there are corrugated sheets for the slow worms and adders to sleep beneath, so it is always worth lifting them gently to see what's underneath – but please replace the log that holds the sheet down.

Spring and early summer is also a good time for the birds that like the woodland fringes. In April and May the greater spotted woodpecker hammers away in the trees, and chiffchaffs, song thrushes, wood warblers, willow warblers, nightingales and blackcaps can be heard, even if they are difficult to see. Blackcaps in particular dislike being seen and however close to your right ear the sweetness of the trilling coming from a bush, it is difficult to spot a bird that is smaller than a sparrow and lacks distinguishable features other than the jet black top of the male's head or the chestnut cap of the female.

The wood and willow warblers are two more sweet singers, and if you hear a rushing downward scale of liquid music, ending with a little upward flourish, you are probably listening to a willow warbler. Visually, there is a better chance of identifying the larger wood warbler thanks to its yellow throat and breast and the yellow stripe over the eyes. As spring progresses, spotted flycatchers arrive and the chance of some clear sightings are good since this is a bird that appears unbothered by humans and perches on a branch waiting to dash out in pursuit of its insect prey. But where there are small birds, that efficient hunter, the sparrowhawk, may well put in an appearance, soaring above the reserve on open wings to reveal the dark brown and white bars distinguishing the female or the chestnut and white bars of the smaller male, before swooping at speed on folded wings if it sees the opportunity for lunch or supper.

But it is butterflies that are at the centre of things here; most of all, perhaps, the ones that rejoice in the beautiful name fritillary. Indeed, the reserve is coppiced on a 12-year cycle specifically to provide the conditions that appeal to the silver-washed fritillary (*Argynnis paphia*) and the small pearl-bordered fritillary (*Boloria selene*). Both have wings that, when open, are a golden orange-brown (on the silver-washed brighter in the male than the female) and heavily freckled with black spots and chevrons, the silver-washed being much the larger of the two butterflies. Why then, one may well ask, are they called silver-washed and pearl-bordered? The answer lies in the under wings, the rear pair being, respectively, 'washed' with silver or pearl. The silver-washed fritillary is found only within south and south-west England and Ireland, and you are most likely to see it in the woodland that is its preferred habitat.

The small pearl-bordered fritillary seems to be doing well in Scotland and Wales, but is declining rapidly in England, and Park Corner Heath is the best of the all-too-few places to find it in Sussex. Unlike the silver-washed, it enjoys grassy habitats such as moorlands and clearings in woods where you are likely to see it in late May and June and again in August, flitting low to the ground looking for its nectar from brambles, thistles and wild flowers such as the knapweed, self heal, red clover and pimpernel that are present on the reserve.

The other species regarded as key on this important reserve are the grizzled skipper (*Pyrgus malvae*) and the white admiral (*Limentis camilla*) and both have distinctive markings. The former is small, an inch (2.5 cm) across, and black and white like a checkerboard. It is one of our earlier butterflies to emerge in mid April and flies about at some speed feeding, in early summer, on bramble flowers, dog rose, tormentil, agrimony and the like. Unless it is alongside a peacock butterfly, the white admiral almost qualifies for the word spectacular. Its ground colour is also black but with a broad white stripe across the wings.

Of the more common butterflies that delight the layman if not the specialist, peacocks are plentiful and, it seems, almost ever present, being seen any time from February to June and then again, as the newly hatched insects emerge, from late July well into the autumn. Of all butterflies they are the most handsome and easily recognised with four bold blue, white and black spots on their red wings. Red admirals are almost as recognisable with a bright red bar on each wing and these migrants from Africa and Europe can, like the peacock, be seen at almost any time of the year. The painted lady is another visitor from Africa, and although its numbers and time of arrival fluctuate from one year to the next they, too, can often be seen much of the time.

And then there are commas most of the year, with scalloped yellow, red and black wings looking almost as though they had been carelessly torn from the pages of a book; orange tips (May and June) with, as the name suggests, large orange tips to their white wings; the bright yellow brimstone, one of the earliest to emerge each year; the small brown argus (May to September) with white-fringed brown wings carrying orange dots around the edges; and the delightfully named gatekeeper which is numerous in July and August.

It would be unfeeling to leave Park Corner Heath without mentioning the other colourful inhabitants, the dragonflies and damselflies that are abundant in summer and early autumn. In early May, the well-named broad-bodied chasers (the males bright blue and the females yellow), emperor and downy emerald dragonflies are on the go, and so are azure, large red and common blue damselflies. By the time summer is at its peak the hawkers, southern and migrant, are on the reserve and will still be there in the autumn, together with common and ruddy darters, emerald damselflies and black-tailed skimmers, whose males are blue and the females yellow-brown, but both of whom have marked black tips to their bodies. In short, Park Corner Heath is very rewarding for those who like nature on the wing and colourful.

Getting there   National grid ref. TQ516147
❯ Off the A22, Uckfield-Upper Dicker road, 2 miles (3 km) south of Halland.

Seasonal highlights
◂ *Spring*: reptiles emerge; early butterfly species: speckled wood, green-veined white, brimstone, holly blue, etc.
◂ *Summer*: height of activity, with over 20 species; dragonflies and damselflies.
◂ *Autumn*: late-flying species; small heath, comma, peacock, small copper, red admiral, etc. still out and about.
◂ *Winter*: first butterflies may appear late winter – brimstones, peacocks, etc.

ERIDGE ROCKS

A MINIATURE RAINFOREST

However many times you visit Eridge Rocks, they stick in the memory. The first of the great rocks confronts you as you turn into the little car park at its foot, and it is the sentinel guarding a long line of sandstone cliffs up to 30 feet (10 m) high. If you have a lively imagination you may picture these rocks forming the bed of a shallow river 135 million years ago, with a herd of dinosaurs – iguanodon, perhaps – standing in the water or drinking at the bank. In their day, though, the rocks of Eridge had yet to be revealed as the cliffs we see now. The present shallow valley below them was washed out as the climate changed in the wake of the ice age a mere 10,000 or so years ago, generating great bodies of turbulent water.

There is no better time to visit Eridge than on a sharp winter's day when the summer leaves that screen the rocks have fallen, when all their crevices and crannies are revealed and when, climate change permitting, the overhangs drip icicles. Yet as recently as 1997 you would have been hard pressed to see the rocks at any time of year. Sussex may have much for which to thank the Victorians, but what they did to this site is not among them. They were much taken with the romantic possibilities of Eridge and tried to enhance it by introducing many species new to it: giant larches, pines, firs, occasional bamboo stands, locust trees and *Rhododendron ponticum*. This was not the harmless garden cultivar, but a wild import of deadly habits that loved the acid soil and spread its millions of seeds for up to a mile whilst poisoning the surrounding soil with its toxic leaves. The Victorians, however, were pleased with the effects since, in those early days, the rhododendron had yet to reveal its potential for controlling everything, and elaborate picnics at the base of the rocks in the shade of the growing larches were among the pleasures our great-grandparents enjoyed. But by the end of the 20th century the enormity of the situation was all too apparent. The rhododendron had coalesced into an almost impenetrable mass towering above the cliffs and covering half the 100-acre (40-hectare) site.

All the time there was a micro-world of great rarity trying to grow on the rock surfaces and in the crevices and its life was in danger when, as the new century opened, the bulldozers moved in to get rid of *Rhododendron ponticum* and reveal what one writer has called 'a miniature rainforest'. It is an astonishing array of mosses, ferns, liverworts and lichens that thrive (rhododendron willing) in the unusual conditions provided by rocks that have hard skins but soft, moisture-absorbent centres. Damp conditions were therefore never a problem for the mosses and their cousins but it is during the winter that they grow, for then the deciduous trees that shield them from the summer sun shed their leaves and let in the light they need for growth. The rhododendron forest, being evergreen, was shutting out this vital winter ingredient.

Mosses and ferns may not be the most spectacular players on the wildlife stage, however much they excite specialists, but two of them in particular are worth a small surge of Sussex pride if only for their rarity in much of England – *Orthodontium gracile* (slender thread moss) is one, and the other is best known by its English name, the Tunbridge filmy fern (*Hymenophyllum tunbrigense*, which is really a moss). Larger than most mosses, this jewel-green specimen has delicate little fern-like leaves hanging down one over the other, quivering almost imperceptibly if a light breeze stirs them, like a modest maiden aunt recounting a minor triumph over the tea cups.

The rocks, mosses, ferns, liverworts and lichens are Eridge's principal claims to fame, and it is no modest claim as there are those who believe it is the most important habitat in the south-east. But by no means everyone has their pulse rate quickened to danger levels at the mention of a liverwort, not even a nationally scarce one such as *Cephalozia umbrosa*, so it is as well that these forms of wildlife are by no means the sum of Eridge's attractions.

The track from the car park will take you more than 650 yards (600 m) along the base of the sandstone cliffs before allowing you to turn uphill to the left and, by turning left again, take the path back among the ancient beech trees, yew and holly that grow atop the cliffs, perhaps making occasional forays to the edge of the rocks to enjoy the view. Or you can turn off the main track to the right, down into the shallow valley beneath the cliffs, and enjoy an afternoon's stroll through pleasant woodland. Alder trees line the stream and the circular path loops round through the oaks, birch, conifers and the old chestnut coppices to regain the main north-south track. In unexpected places you will probably notice clearings. These are where the invasive rhododendron was so dense that nothing else grew and following the resultant clearance the newly-opened areas were replanted with oak and hazel to help the woodland back to its pre-Victorian state. Some of our ancestors' importations, though, have been left or replaced as they begin to decay – some of the giant larches below the rocks, for example. They add to the appearance of the wood without threatening other forms of wildlife, so why not?

At many times of the year you will be assailed by birdsong as you walk, for almost all the varieties of tits are to be found here, as well as nuthatches, treecreepers and green woodpeckers. In the winter and early spring you will probably hear the drumming of greater spotted woodpeckers and, before the leaves are back on the trees, you may well see one – and hear two! Rather than proclaim their rights to a territory (or their attractions to a female) through song, as most birds do, greater spotted woodpeckers drum on the tree trunk, in bursts of five or six seconds at a time. Then they pause and wait for an answering drum roll from elsewhere in the wood before replying – or flying off to investigate, depending on the language of the answer. If you catch sight of one in flight, you will recognise it from the black and white bars across the wings and the prominent white shoulder patches. In the autumn, flocks of long-tailed tits and siskins gather to feed along the margins of the stream, where they are usually joined by bands of pushy little goldfinches, who seem to think their pretty red faces, white cheeks, black heads and black and yellow barred wings, give them the right to push and shove like lager louts on a Friday night!

The woodland flowers of spring are here in abundance, with bluebells well to the fore as in so many parts of Sussex. The summer is rich in butterflies, without attracting any rarities of note. The fact that these things are so is thanks – in part – to the coppicing of hazel and chestnut trees that used to be done, the evidence for which is still apparent. Why trees are coppiced is a question asked with surprising frequency. On the one hand the life of the tree is prolonged by periodically cutting its main trunk down to a little above ground level and renewing its energy so that it throws up multiple stems; on the other, more light is allowed into the coppiced areas, encouraging the grasses and wild flowers to bloom which, in turn, bring the insects, butterflies and birds. And as an incidental bonus, both hazel and chestnut are very useful woods when cut, the one being whippy and pliable, the other having water-resistant durability, qualities valued in an age before technical wizardry but still with their uses today.

The rocks, though, remain in all seasons. Wherever you wander in this attractive site your steps lead you back to them, and they leave their haunting presence in the memory. The Victorians may unwittingly have caused them to be overgrown and obscured, but one can understand their fascination with this place very well.

Getting there   National grid ref. TQ554355
❷ Off the A26 from Crowborough towards Tunbridge Wells.

Seasonal highlights
🍂 *Spring*: birds, including the less-common marsh tit.
🍂 *Summer*: butterflies in good numbers.
🍂 *Autumn*: siskins, long tailed tits and goldfinches in large flocks.
🍂 *Winter*: the rocks unmasked.

BROADWATER WARREN

WORK IN PROGRESS

Here is a priceless chance to watch a new wildlife reserve in the making or, more accurately, in the restoring. In January 2007 the RSPB completed the purchase of 450 acres (180 hectares) of Broadwater Forest and the Warren, a mixture of ancient woodland and commercial conifer plantations with small patches of heathland hanging on between the trees. The intention is to restore it, over a decade, to a High Weald landscape of open heath interspersed with stands of ancient trees and scattered conifers, and so attract back some of our valuable, rarer wildlife whilst providing a place of tranquillity and beauty for human visitors.

Early medieval kings reserved four great forests in the Sussex High Weald for their hunting enjoyment – and by forest they did not mean closely crowded trees, but open heaths across which they could chase their quarry when it had been flushed from the nearby woodlands. Broadwater Warren is a fragment of one of these royal forests. Nearer to our time, old maps bear witness that, in the 19th century, this was still largely lowland heath – a habitat which, by the latter half of the 20th century, had become a rare commodity. This is not to deny the attractions of the reserve even as it is, before restoration work has started; but the spaces between the dense conifer plantations and the deciduous woods have been so overwhelmed by birch and pine scrub, mostly greater than head height, that only now and again can a tall man glimpse what is beyond.

Yet the land is gently undulating, falling southwards to pond and stream along the valley bottom before climbing again on the other side. For the moment one can only imagine the stunning vistas that would be there if one could only escape the densely packed birch and pine saplings that block the views.

Good footpaths intercut the reserve, bordered by narrow, scrub-free verges in which are dotted occasional pimpernel, St John's wort, knapweed, burdock, bird's foot trefoil, teasel and agrimony; and, here and there, are the pinks and purples of bell heather and ling. The words 'occasional' and 'here and there' alert you to the problem. These are plants that are hanging on, almost but not quite – for now – over-whelmed by the loss of their habitat wrought by the expanding scrub and the dark conifer plantations. One that has been lost was known on this site until recently, a native flower of Britain that is now in the red data book of endangered species – hairy greenweed (*Genista pilosa*), a close relative of the uncommon beauty, dyer's greenweed (*see p.51*, Bedelands Farm). Like its cousin, it is clustered with masses of pea-like golden flowers in June and July, and takes its name from the hairs on its young leaves that disappear as it matures. Unlike dyer's greenweed, however, it needs dry, acid soil and plenty of light, a commodity denied it by the overwhelming scrub.

What, then, can we expect to see as work on the site progresses between 2008 and 2018, and to what can we look forward when the labour is done? For a start, an army of volunteers will be needed to help the specialists. There are surveys to be carried out to establish exactly what is there at the moment. Are there, for example, rare ferns and fungi, mosses and liverworts in the floor of the valley, maybe along the banks of the stream that tumbles over sandstone rocks, or perhaps around the brackish pools and in the mire that surrounds them? Are there uncommon insects and invertebrates at home there? At the same time the dense rhododendron obliterating the sandstone must be cleared. This is the same sandstone to be found at nearby Eridge Rocks (*see p.64*), and it is the same fiercesome *Rhododendron ponticum* that is on the rampage, so the labour will be herculean.

Next will come the first phase of clearing the scrub and removing part of the brooding conifer plantations, within which there is little light and beneath which little grows save bracken, grass and the occasional bramble, and then but sparsely. These, after all, were convenience trees, planted to make money from logging. There is no disguising the fact that, for the human visitor, there will be sections of the reserve that do not look pretty in the immediate aftermath of clearance. The initial reward will be views that begin to open northwards up the slope of the valley, and east and west across undulating land, to the belts of ancient woodland that will remain.

In other respects the first fruits of these labours will show themselves quickly. Heather seeds remain dormant for more than 50 years and, as on Stedham Common, once light reaches them they germinate and burst into life. Within a year of being cleared, an area overrun by scrub will begin to turn pink and purple as drifts of bell heather and ling start to colonise it. Clumps of gorse will begin to spread their spikes, and the wild flowers that are currently confined to narrow verges will have their opportunity to intermingle with the heather. To help them out, livestock will be brought in to graze the coarser grasses that might otherwise overwhelm the flowers. As a result, butterflies of heath and woodland fringe will soon be taking advantage.

Butterflies that used to be here include three that are uncommon or endangered, and are now to be found in only one or two places in Sussex – the silver-studded blue (see p.17, Iping & Stedham Commons), the pearl-bordered and the small pearl-bordered fritillaries (see p.61-2, Park Corner Heath). Whether they can be persuaded back, only time and patience will tell, but insects will certainly multiply and that will bring a variety of birds and dragonflies. One fascinating insect found only in the south-east in England is already here, the slave-making ant (*Formica sanguinea*). These anti-social creatures execute mass raids on the nests of other ants, carrying off the larvae that then grow up to a lifetime of drudgery, feeding and tending their slave-making mistresses.

As at Eridge Rocks, flocks of siskins, goldfinches and tits are likely to twitter and feed in numbers along the banks of the main stream that bisects the reserve once the lowering conifers that currently overhang the southern side of the valley have gone. One of the reserve's most interesting features, however, is the mire that spreads along part of the valley floor. Mire is peaty land that holds the water and in which dead plant material accumulates. It is an unusual habitat in Sussex and since 1991 some species have disappeared from it – marsh gentian, bog asphodel and round-leaved sundew, for example, though not, one hopes, irretrievably. Others that love wet acidic marshes are still to be found, such as marsh violet, with its attractive lilac flowers from April to July; cotton grass; and tussock sedge, that can grow over the years into dense clumps of dark green, fine-bladed foliage. Another rare plant here, usually found in mountains, is lemon-scented fern (*Oreoptoris limbosperma*).

One hopes for uncommon visitors on the restored heathland up the eastern slope and on the western flank: woodlarks, for example; Dartford warblers; and a little bird that has declined in Britain by 90 per cent, the lesser redpoll (*Carduelis cabaret*). As they have catholic tastes, preferring birch seeds but happily devouring insects and the seeds of willowherb, dandelion, chickweed and so on, there is a good chance they will find restored Broadwater Warren to their liking but, with the lesser redpoll, you can never be sure…

Creating a new nature reserve is a complex business and exact plans for Broadwater Warren have to be determined after public consultation, detailed surveys and an Environmental Impact Assessment. The reserve will not be launched by the RSPB until a proper car park, intended for September 2008, has been built but, to preserve the tranquillity of this place, there are no plans for a visitor centre.

Getting there   National grid ref. TQ5536
⦿ The Groombridge road, off the A26 Crowborough-Tunbridge Wells.

Seasonal highlights

◖ *Spring*: birds of heath and woodland fringes (especially woodlarks, tree pipits and Dartford warblers); wood ants emerging.

◖ *Summer*: heathers and wild flowers; butterflies and dragonflies on restored pool; nightjars churring at dusk; autumn colours.

◖ *Autumn*: late butterflies and dragonflies; stonechats and migrating birds.

◖ *Winter*: siskins and redpolls in birch and alder; flocks of tits in woods and along stream.

LULLINGTON HEATH

HIGH ON CHALK

You are not going to call this the experience of a lifetime. That would be too much. But as you stand on Fore Down, at the north-west corner of Lullington Heath, you will be hard pressed not to believe you are looking at a classical view of England, one that stays in the memory when you are stuck in a traffic jam or in some corner of a foreign field. To the north, rounded plateaux shorten the view in the direction of the Long Man of Wilmington; in the distant north-west stretch the wooded slopes of the High Weald; and to the west the steep north face of Firle Beacon heralds the glorious sweep of the South Downs to the western horizon. It is pointless to debate whether the views from the crown of Levin Down or the ridge of Bow Hill above Kingley Vale are finer. It is enough that you are here, privileged to enjoy such breath-taking beauty on some hopes a day of rolling white clouds high in a blue sky. Yet there is more, much more, to enjoy, for you are on rare and treasured land — a National Nature Reserve that is the largest area of chalk heath in Britain.

To reach it you leave the picturesque village of Jevington, nestling in a narrow downland combe behind Beachy Head, by the South Downs Way past the small church and two large fields before climbing through a woodland fringe mainly of horse chestnuts and sycamores. Here and there a rabbit may skip across your path, an unusually welcome sign because, although they wreak havoc on some reserves, on this one they play a vital role, alongside the Exmoor ponies and Hebridean and Welsh Beulah sheep that graze the heath, in keeping the grass short for the flowers to bloom. Keep straight on over the crosspaths and turn left at a T-junction shortly afterwards to climb the chalk track for 200-300 yards (180-270 m) before you come, suddenly it seems, onto the open crest of the hill. After one more field you are on the reserve itself.

Lullington Heath is in the shape of a rough rhomboid and you are at its north-east corner, where a map presents you with two choices – to turn down onto the Heath and walk diagonally across it, carrying on round the perimeter path; or to keep straight on along the white chalk track and do everything in reverse. If the latter, the views across the downs, already sublime, will be even better as you climb up to Fore Down in the distance, where an additional pleasure awaits, only a few yards off the path. Winchester Pond is a 19th-century dewpond, encircled by a windbreak of hawthorn and gorse. On a high summer's day it is a perfect place to relax in the sun, while the ever-present breeze rustles the bulrushes that fringe the pond and dragonflies hover above the water. Great crested newts inhabit the pond between March and June and, although they are mainly nocturnal, you might glimpse them as they rise briefly but periodically to the surface. Great crested newts are a protected species and, contrary to popular belief, spend much of their life on land, especially the males who are the ones with the crest. In September they look for crevices under stones and logs, or in walls, in which to hibernate.

If you have elected to turn down across the heath, saving Fore Down and Winchester Pond for later, you will be struck at once by the scattered gorse bushes and hawthorn trees, wind-shaped and stunted, but most of all, in summer, by the great splashes of vivid purple heather that seem to clothe the heath. Then you will start to see the flowers – first, perhaps, the striking purple-blue flower, flecked with long red stamens like hungry tongues, of the strangely named viper's bugloss. Herbalists in the 17th century decided that it was 'a most singular remedy against poison and the sting of scorpions' on no better evidence than that 'its stalk was speckled like a snake or viper'. To our eyes it is a cheerful, handsome plant, blooming freely from June into the autumn, and beloved of bees and butterflies.

Viper's bugloss is one among a great many wild flowers thrusting themselves up for our attention, some more obvious than others. There is marjoram, salad burnet, the lilac blue of wild thyme and the tiny yellow stars of tormentil – acid-loving flowers growing happily alongside the alkaline chalk-dwellers. And this is what makes chalk heath so unusual. As on parts of Levin Down, wind-blown acidic soils settled on top of the chalk thousands of years ago during the last Ice Age, allowing plants that would not normally be found together to feel quite at home in each other's company. In many places, this unusual combination has been lost to ploughing for agriculture or to invasion by scrub. Only in one or two less accessible spots has the heath been grazed continuously by rabbits and farmed animals. Ponies, sheep and rabbits are not the only ones that nibble a living here – so too does a herd of Bagot goats. They are wild in the sense that they are not farmed for milk or meat, but partly tame because they are sometimes given a lunchtime snack, and if you are on the heath around the middle of the day you may be startled to hear a raucous calling in place of a lunch bell followed by the sight of a scampering pack of brown-and-white goats.

Dotted everywhere in the longer grasses are the bubbling yellow tresses of lady's bedstraw, the reddish trumpets of calamint and the yellow spires of mignonette whilst, from the cropped turf, the cheering pink of scarlet pimpernels and the purple-blue of delicate clustered bellflowers smile up at us. We all have our favourites, and I have three: dropwort, with its creamy white petals and yellow stamens, borne on a tall, slender stem; the dwarf thistle, with myriad fluffy purple heads tucked down in the grass; and eyebright, no more than three or four inches high on delicate dusky stems, with pairs of small, dark green, serrated leaves topped by three or four tiny white flowers with precise black lines leading the eye to their yellow centres. There are also the ear-shaped yellow flowers of horseshoe vetch, the favourite food of red-tailed bumble bees and the only food of two butterflies of the chalk grasslands, the adonis blue and the chalkhill blue.

Fifty-four butterfly species have been recorded here and in Friston, the forest that borders Lullington Heath. Red admirals, browns and gatekeepers are common, and dark green fritillaries, grizzled and dingy skippers, brown argus and small coppers are among the frequently seen varieties. In addition to these the silver-spotted skipper, the adonis and chalkhill blues and the grayling are the ones the enthusiasts most want to see. The grayling is historically common on heathland, but on chalk heath and chalk grassland it has subtly adapted its colour to lighter shades for greater protection. It normally flies from June to September unless the summer is wet; in 2007 there were hardly any sightings.

Beachy Head and Cuckmere Haven are favoured routes into Britain for migratory birds and it is no surprise that Lullington Heath, midway between the two, boasts 98 species passing through or settling in the scrub that borders it and is controlled in patches within it. Among the reasons for the heath being a favoured bird habitat is the wealth of insects and spiders that lurk in the grass or gorse. By early summer 2007, 48 species of spider had already been recorded (and more undoubtedly emerged later on), among them the funnelweb and wasp spiders. Poke about in the grass and you will soon find the funnel-shaped web of the former which, as the summer passes, its industrious owner constantly enlarges. The female wasp spider has distinctive yellow and black hoops and, although not native, is Britain's largest arachnid. She makes hollows in the grass over which she spins her web, marked by an unusual zigzag across its centre and then sits back and waits for the grasshopper prey to jump in. Many have looked for it and only a few are chosen to find it, but in August and September it is well worth making the effort to catch a glimpse of this spectacular creature.

Getting there   National grid ref. TQ545016
❷ Take the A2270 Eastbourne-Polegate road, turn south for Jevington.

Seasonal highlights

◖ *Spring: spring flowers; migrating and breeding birds (dawn chorus).*
◖ *Summer: wild flowers and pyramidal orchids; butterflies; wayfaring trees (Viburnum lantana) with spectacular red berry clusters.*
◖ *Autumn: late flowers; butterflies; migrating birds.*
◖ *Winter: the magnificent views in any season.*

FILSHAM REEDBEDS

REED-DWELLERS DELIGHT

This is not an easy reserve to find. If coming by car you need your wits about you and your eyesight at its sharpest to find the car park, a narrow entrance on the north side of the A259 Hastings-Bexhill road just west of the junction with Harley Shute Road. In the car park you are confronted by a rubbish tip, but be not dismayed. Things can only get better and they do. Take the gravelled path straight ahead, then follow the signed footpath to Crowhurst and Worsham along the river bank. You will be shadowed by smart little static caravans on the other side of the river, but it is worth telling yourself that the owners of both the caravan park and the waste disposal site have been helpful and encouraging to the nature reserve.

In summer, butterflies dance attendance as you walk and the white flower and lily-like pads of frogbit dot the surface of the slow-moving river inching its way to the sea at Bulverhythe. Before long, the caravans have been left behind and willow and reed have replaced them. This is the beginning of the reserve, and half way along its western flank a wooden bridge gives access to it. Over the bridge turn left and in 40 yards (37 m) a boardwalk leads into the heart of a secret world of water and reeds, home to a great many birds.

There is no escaping the fact that this is a highly specialised reserve, catering mostly for reed-dwelling birds and therefore appealing mainly to enthusiasts. Yet Filsham is not without other attractions and the person whose interest in wildlife is a general delight in natural beauty will still find it appealing. There is a public footpath that skirts the northern and eastern flanks and a walk along it provides beguiling views up Combe Haven valley and a clearer idea of how the reedbeds came to be here in the first place. But first, a word of warning. The path does not describe a complete circle, so you will have to turn back on reaching the higher grassland at the south-east corner if you are not to lose yourself in an almost impenetrable tangle of blackthorn, hawthorn and bramble.

If you decide to take this perimeter walk, it is best not to enter the reserve by the bridge half way along its western side. Instead, continue with the river on your right and cross a second bridge at the north-west corner. Willow and hawthorn screen the reedbeds at the core, with only occasional glimpses inward through small gaps, but the view outwards up the shallow valley is clear, and more reeds stretch north along its floor. The whole valley bottom was once pasture but, as grazing died out and nearby suburban housing estates were built, the water levels rose and the reedbeds formed. It is a rare example, however accidental, of human activity creating a wildlife sanctuary rather than destroying one. Nevertheless, the difficulty of access and the initial lack of control over the water levels resulted in the dead leaves and stems of the reeds themselves choking the stretches of open water. By the 1990s the reedbeds were close to dying and the work of restoration has been going on for a decade – opening up drainage ditches, inserting sluice gates to control water flows, removing willow that was clumping together to obscure the light and cutting and clearing reeds. Where firmer ground meets the water, banks have been profiled to give shallower slopes for the wading birds that forage along the margin for insects and small fish.

As you return to the reedbeds, keep an eye open in early summer for yellow flag iris and ragged robin, a wild member of the Lychnis family with appealing, higgledy-piggledy narrow red petals. Later in the summer, the yellows, whites and blues of meadow rue, meadow-sweet and marsh woundwort take over. Most of all it is worth looking out for the water-loving flowers that flourish in the first half of summer wherever light strikes the ditches – frogbit, water violet and the extraordinary bladderwort, a plant that floats on the surface, throwing up a yellow flower 6 to 8 inches (15 to 20 cm) high but which, below the surface, is busily devouring tiny marine insects with small oval leaves that look like miniature bladders. The more open the water the more dragonflies there will be and there is a good mixture of these, including the red-eyed damselfly (*see p.18*, Iping Common) and the infrequently seen hairy dragonfly. This is the smallest of the hawkers and flies early in the summer, from May to early July, before the bigger hawkers are up and about. The male has blue dots, and the female yellow, on a mainly black body.

Where there are dragonflies there are sure to be swallows and martins chasing them in autumn, and in their turn they will be pursued by birds of prey, lightning-quick hobbies in particular. Sparrowhawks are plentiful in the area and display a cunning that is chilling to behold. A bird may take refuge in the depths of an oak tree whilst a sparrowhawk glides by, apparently oblivious to the presence of its prey. But wait! Even as the smaller bird is thinking it has escaped detection, the hunter wheels about and plunges through the screening leaves to pluck it from its branch. In winter the marsh harriers arrive, swooping across the very reeds they have come to roost in. And it is the birds, of all sorts, that demand top billing at Filsham.

A few of the reed dwellers are willing to show themselves flitting above the vegetation but for much the greater number the dense blanket of reeds provides the watery secrecy they crave. Among the former are the bearded tits, the outrageously handsome male sporting a lavender blue head and neck, orange-brown wings with black and white stripes and a black moustache of such laughable proportions – practically a walrus – that it was taken to be a beard, and the bird was named accordingly. For the most part, however, the birds are here for privacy although the warblers cannot resist a good song so you may well hear what you cannot see. Cetti's warbler breeds here and throughout the year its song – described as 'an almost explosive series of liquid notes' – is powerful and far-reaching. From deep within the reeds the sedge warbler sings its heart out by day and sometimes by night, in long and rapid phrases. Of the warblers only the reed warbler disappoints, chattering unmusically. You probably have a better chance of glimpsing a reed bunting since this bird climbs the reed stem or even perches on a bush, before letting rip with its simple series of chirps. It is again the male that has the distinctive appearance with a black head and throat encircled by a wide white collar.

Among the birds you will be even more fortunate to see, though winter is probably your best chance, is the water rail, which keeps to the bottom of the reeds, slipping easily between the stems with its slender body. And if the water rail is shy it is as nothing compared to an occasional summer or autumn visitor, the bittern or, to give it one of its endearing popular names, the butterbump. Bitterns do not, alas, breed here. They are, rightly and understandably, fussy about their requirements for this crucial activity. The site must be large enough to provide good fishing and, like a senior citizen contemplating the morning bath, the water must be just the right depth. Filsham's is not deep enough to satisfy these exacting needs and so, whilst they are happy to drop in for a week or two's visit, you will have to go to Rye Harbour (*see p.84*) to hear the booming mating call of the suppliant male.

An even rarer visitor has been observed here. The spotted crake (*Porzana porzana*) is a spring migrant that bestows its favours on a bare handful of spots in Britain, and less than 20 breeding pairs are known, but it seems that Filsham has been added to its list. It is as secretive as the bittern, and dawn and dusk are the times to catch a glimpse of a bird no bigger than a starling that flies with fluttering wings and trailing legs. But we can hardly complain that these denizens of marsh and reed remain so deeply hidden. This is their world. We are the privileged visitors.

Getting there   National grid ref. TQ775097
🜂 Off the A259 Hastings-Bexhill road.

Seasonal highlights
🜂 *Spring: migrating birds arriving or passing through.*
🜂 *Summer: dragonflies; marsh flowers.*
🜂 *Autumn: migrating birds passing through and swallows, martins, hobbies.*
🜂 *Winter: marsh harriers.*

MARLINE WOODS & MEADOWS
HIDDEN TREASURE

Marline is not easy to find so some words of explanation may be helpful. The B2029, Queensway, acts like a ring road round the north-west side of Hastings and Marline borders its western edge. There are no parking facilities and the only option is to park in Napier Road, which is wide enough to allow this where it joins Queensway. There are two access footpaths, both off busy Queensway. One is about 400 yards (370 m) south (left) of the junction with Napier Road; the other just a few yards north of the same junction. The latter path runs alongside the boundary fence of the Queensway Business Park. With concern for the environment rapidly climbing the list of political and popular concerns as the 21st century opens, one would have expected most local councils to go to some lengths to protect a wildlife reserve of considerable natural beauty that is designated a Site of Special Scientific Interest. Hastings Borough Council, on the contrary, seems proud of itself for planning to develop 16,000 square metres of office space and light industry right up against it. Such vandalism seems incredible, but it is on the way to becoming fact.

Suppress your outrage — if you can — as the footpath leaves it behind and you enjoy the calming sensation of passing through a small meadow and dropping down into Marline Wood at the northern end of the reserve. The reserve is a mosaic of interconnecting flower-rich meadows and woods (Four Acre Wood and Park Wood being the other two) stretching southwards along the side of a valley that steepens into a ghyll. The stream that meanders along the bottom defines the western boundary of the reserve.

In Marline Wood beech and oak are the main contributors to the soothing, peaceful canopy that shades the stream as it burbles over little sandstone falls. The ferns, mosses and liverworts along the banks are the principal reasons for the reserve's SSSI status, but the springtime flowers are the greater attraction for most visitors. Wood anemone, bluebells, celandine, primroses and violets bloom here and so do marsh marigolds (or molly-blobs to give them a local name) and wild garlic. If you are a summertime visitor, it is worth following the path over the stream for a few yards in order to glance into two meadows that are not part of the reserve. The lack of flowers in these untended fields will make a strong contrast with the meadows you will shortly be entering.

The main path southwards through Marline Wood stays just above the point where the slopes of the ghyll start to fall sharply away, and a rustic fence of brush encourages you to keep to the track to protect life and limb so that you are still intact as you emerge into the first of the flower-bedecked meadows. At first glance one might think this palette splashed with colour is how all our fields might look if left alone to get on with it. In reality it is not many years since these meadows were choked with bracken and bramble and threatening to eliminate some of the rarer species of grass and flowers. The tide was turned by the hard work of volunteers clearing the terrain, followed by an annual pattern of cutting for hay and then grazing, that has given us today's flower-rich meadows. Indeed in the second half of summer you may well see British whites or Sussex cattle browsing the coarser grasses to create space for next spring's finer plants, their tails swishing the air like bovine maestri conducting an orchestra of flies.

The result is a symphony of colourful flowers throughout the summer months. The cuckooflower is the harbinger of what is to follow – treading on its heels come red campion, common spotted orchids, adders tongue fern, rare dyer's greenweed (*see p.51*, Bedelands Farm) and yellow rattle, so named because of the rattle the dry seed pods make in late summer. The second half of summer brings St John's wort, red clover, bird's foot trefoil, tufted vetch, self heal, tormentil, cranes-bill and spear thistle, with yellow spires of agrimony waving above the grass. Then, as the lazy days of high summer merge into the early days of autumn, the bright yellows and deep reds and purples of fleabane, knapweed and marsh woundwort reach up to demand the walker's admiration. Some of these common names are reminders of the way our forefathers regarded plants as valuable for their uses, often medic-inal, rather than their beauty. Fleabane deterred fleas; St John's wort was used to heal ulcers, sores and internal wounds; tormentil relieved the griping pains of intestinal infections; and self-heal, like yarrow and woundwort, stemmed blood after accidents, for which reason it was sometimes know as the carpenter's herb. Medieval physicians and wise women would have had a busy time harvesting for their lotions and powders in Marline's meadows.

As you would expect, butterflies adore this abundance of nectar. Whereas the woodlands are home to purple hairstreaks, commas and white admirals, the meadows teem with ringlets, green hairstreaks, orange tips, gatekeepers, meadow browns and red admirals, with the white admiral emerging from the trees to browse the margins on calm, sunny days. It is in these margins where scrub and bramble hug the edges of the woods and especially where there may be coppiced hazel and chestnut nearby that dormice are happiest. Alas, your chances of seeing this shy but endearing little creature are slim, since it is nocturnal and hibernates from October to April.

The scrub and bramble play host to birds as well — nuthatches, whitethroats, blackcaps, bullfinches and occasionally another retiring character — the hawfinch. Although fairly well spread across England, hawfinches are not often seen in Sussex. They like woodland but particu-larly appreciate hornbeam and this may be the clue to their presence at Marline, for Park Wood has old, coppiced hornbeam, although whether the bird is actually breeding there is not yet proven. Nightingales also love ancient, coppiced hornbeam as well as hazel, ash and sweet chest-nut, and in the woods both greater and lesser spotted woodpeckers are to be found. The former is easy enough to see and hear as it hammers on a tree trunk between March and May, though it will hastily scramble round the back of the trunk if it spots you watching it. The lesser spotted woodpecker on the other hand (*see p.32*, Burton Pond) makes the shy hawfinch look like a Hollywood starlet on Oscar night, so anxious is it not to be seen.

No mention of the less common species of flora and fauna would be complete, though, without mentioning an orchid of the woodlands, the violet helleborine (*Epipactis purpurata*). This, too, likes hazel and hornbeam coppice on clay soils. It is confined to scattered sites in the south and south-east but where it settles it has the strength to force its way through a tarmac road surface. It can grow to a height of 2 feet (60 cm), generally in clusters of stems with a multitude of flowers, predominantly green but with an attractive pale pink and brown lip. So why violet helleborine? Because its first shoots are a light violet colour and even when fully grown it retains the colour at the base of the leaf.

In short, there is something of pleasure, whether common or unusual, at almost any time of the year as you wander through the interlaced woods and meadows. And this is without mentioning the beauty of the view from the top of the meadows across the broad, wooded valley to a typically English scene of copse, hedgerow and field with the white cone of an oast house completing the scene. Nor, for fear of repeating what is in the chapter on Lullington Heath, have I mentioned Britain's largest non-native arachnid, the colourful wasp spider, that is here in the meadows making its cunning little trap for insouciant grasshoppers in late summer.

Getting there   National grid ref. TQ784122
◉ B2092 (Queensway), west of junction of A2100 and A21.

Seasonal highlights
◀ *Spring*: woodland wild flowers.
◀ *Summer*: wild flowers in the meadows; birds; butterflies.
◀ *Autumn*: late summer wild flowers; mosses, ferns and liverworts.
◀ *Winter*: winter woodland; mosses and liverworts.

RYE HARBOUR & CASTLE WATER

SHINGLE & BITTERNS

From the knoll on which it stands, the historic town of Rye looks south towards the sea, 2 miles (3 km) distant, across a triangle of land enclosed by the rivers Brede to the west, and Rother to the east. Within the triangle lie the interconnected nature reserves of Rye Harbour and Castle Water, to which an excellent free guide is available from the Information Centre near the Rye Harbour village car park. As you stand among Castle Water's broad fields, grazing sheep, scattered trees and nearby reedbeds, your first thought might be to wonder at the almost abrupt contrast between the two sites. Second thoughts bring different and opposite perceptions. As you notice the ridges across the fields, realisation dawns that Castle Water is actually an almost seamless transition from Rye Harbour and that what links them is shingle and water.

In Tudor times Rye was a harbour of strategic importance standing next to the sea but, for the last 400 years, periodic storms and tempests have thrown up great banks of shingle. There are man-made testaments marking the steady process of separating Rye from the sea that once lapped beneath its walls. In the first half of the 16th century, Henry VIII built here an artillery castle of near perfect symmetry to guard the coast. Now Camber Castle keeps solitary watch over a field, scarcely within earshot of the sea. Above the car park, similarly stranded, stands a Martello tower, erected during the Napoleonic wars; and, among the shingle near the shore, are two gaunt World War II blockhouses, built in case of invasion through nearby Camber Sands. Slowly, specialist plants have colonised the shingle, soil has accumulated in and over it, hosting a succession of vegetation the diversity of which increases as the triangle narrows to its apex below the town.

Shingle – gravel – is an invaluable commodity. It has been excavated here for generations but nowadays receives protection as a special wildlife habitat. As excavation ceased, the pits filled with water – the second element that dominates the site – and across the nature reserve there are saline lagoons, wader pools, areas of saltmarsh and freshwater pits that between them support a great diversity of life. To the casual eye the reserve may appear to be a wild place, left alone for the birds and insects, plants and animals to make use of as they can. The very opposite is true. Almost every square inch of it is managed with one overriding purpose – to benefit about 150 rare species, some of them endangered on a global scale. As a single example, take a gravel pit at the moment it ceases to be worked. It is deep and steep-sided and, before it is of use to more than a tiny handful of species, islands must be built and the sides must be profiled to provide shallows and gradual inclines so that the varying needs of many diverse forms of life can be satisfied. Little grebes and sandwich terns, for instance, nest on islands to escape predators such as foxes and badgers.

The results of this careful attention to detail are most immediately obvious in the wealth of bird life, for birds of sea and shore, fresh water and reed are here in abundance. For those with specialised avian interests this is a paradise in any season, supported by four well-maintained hides containing, for good measure, the yearly breeding records of the species most at home on the reserve.

For those who simply like birds without aspiring to intimate knowledge, the great shingle banks are impressive in any season. As you walk the path between them, the sense of elemental natural power is enhanced by occasional glimpses of a post or two of the old sea defences poking above the shingle, the rest long since overwhelmed by storm and stones.

From distant Dungeness, where the hazy silhouette of the power station looks like an ocean-going vessel, all the way west to Winchelsea (with only the brief interlude of Camber Sands) the shingle-bound coast is a site of European rarity because of the uncommon life this harsh environment sustains. May and June are the best months to visit, when it is awash with the colour of shingle flowers and the sound of thousands of seabirds. There are the pushy, look-at-me plants that want to dominate your attention – sea kale thrusting up great heads of white like would-be cauliflowers; and valerian everywhere, light pink to crimson red. But there are other, more delicate, beauties in abundance: yellow horned-poppy; dainty, ground-hugging herb robert; slender stems of seaside thistle; ivy-leafed toadflax; and stately, handsome viper's bugloss that hosts several rare species of moth. And there is a newcomer – or rather a resurrected old-comer. Stinking hawksbeard (*Crepis foetida*) became extinct in Britain a quarter of a century ago, but has recently been successfully reintroduced on the beach reserve and, in 2007, the yellow flowers were seen again.

Tread carefully on the shingle in May and June, though – or better still not at all – for flowers and moths are not its only inhabitants. Ringed plovers, little terns and oystercatchers consider the stones the perfect camouflage for their nests and eggs, and if their eagle-eyed predators find them hard to spot, a blundering human has no chance! Keep a watchful eye open, too, for wheatears and shelducks that share the uncommon trait of nesting underground in any convenient hole they can find, such as a rabbit burrow.

Thanks to its natural reclamation from the sea, to the succession of vegetation that has spread over its breadth, and to its warm, predominantly dry (but often very windy) climate, Rye Harbour embraces an unusually wide variety of micro-habitats in which many rarities are to be found. Under this heading beetles score particularly well and many are to be found in the drainage ditches or bare patches on the banks around Castle Water. High on the list of uncommon varieties is the mud beetle (*Heterocerus hispidulus*), which, however dull it sounds, has rarity to distinguish it and even today has spread no further than East

Anglia. Pride of place, though, goes to the little spangled button beetle (*Omophron limbatum*), with distinctive green zigzag markings on its silvery-brown carapace in keeping with its cheery name.

As the name implies, Castle Water is dominated by a large, winding freshwater pit with branching arms and channels. With its islands and reedbeds it looks as if it has been here for ever, yet its life as a gravel pit ended only in 1970. As recently as 2003 and 2006 it was greatly enlarged, creating 140 more islands. Among the many beneficiaries are water voles, who are thriving here; and a creature you won't see – unless you inadvisedly plunge into the lake with bare legs – the globally endangered medicinal leech.

You will need to be both dedicated and lucky to see one of our rarest and most secretive birds, the bittern, but it is there, hidden deep in the reeds waiting, motionless, for its prey of eels and rudd. A hundred years ago the bittern was extinct in Britain but, by 2005, 45 breeding pairs were recorded, and one of the many reasons for creating new wetland at Castle Water is to offer better support to breeding bitterns. The dawn hours of a winter's morning offer the best chance of hearing its booming mating call.

But if patience is needed to spot the rarities, there is no shortage of other attractions. Cuckoos love the area, partly because the plentiful reed warblers provide convenient hosts for their eggs, and partly for the ample supply of a favourite food, hairy brown caterpillars. Throughout the summer dragonflies and damselflies skim the surface of the water hunting insects to be, in turn, pursued by swooping swallows and martins – and this, with the inexorable logic of nature, brings the marsh harriers and hobbies flashing across the reserve.

Getting there   National grid ref. TQ942187
◉ Look for Rye Harbour village, off the A259, Winchelsea and Hastings direction.

Seasonal highlights
◂ *Spring*: arrival of summer migrant birds; shingle flowers.
◂ *Summer*: bird song; breeding terns, gulls and waders; orchids; dragonflies; butterflies.
◂ *Autumn*: variety of wading birds; swallows and martins assembling for migration.
◂ *Winter*: smew, bittern and ducks.

URBAN NATURE RESERVES

STANMER & HASTINGS

Three miles (5 km) from the centre of Brighton and immediately west of the University of Sussex, Stanmer Park nestles in a fold of the downs, with wooded slopes rising to east, north and west. It was once the estate of the Earls of Chichester and at its heart is a handsome, early 18th-century palladian house facing a small estate church with wood-shingled spire and, behind that, a village of picturesque cottages and terraced houses, mostly flint dressed.

Stanmer Park is classified as a local nature reserve, though you would hardly guess it as you approach the house and village up a long driveway past carefully landscaped slopes, dotted with specimen trees in the manner of 18th-century landowners intent on displaying their taste and wealth. But since 1947, when Brighton purchased the estate, we have become the legatees and are thus enabled to enjoy another of the features on which earlier landowners lavished their time and money — the extensive woods, and there are three, that clothe the surrounding downs. To the north-east of the house and village is Millbank Wood; to the north-west, Upper Lodge Wood; and rising behind the house to the east is Great Wood, in which the paths are lined in places with erect, towering beech trees. Not all of these, alas, survived the great storm of 1987 that destroyed over two thirds of Stanmer's trees for which the evidence survives in fallen, moss-covered trunks replaced by plenty of much younger growth.

The medley of colours created by the specimen trees as they merge into their woodland background is lovely, but only when you have passed behind the house and village and begun to climb the downland slopes does the sense of unmanaged nature take over. It is a false sense because, in Britain at least, very little landscape is not managed for one purpose or another. In the manner of once great landed estates, the woods here are separated by a patchwork of fields. They are part of two tenant farms that, until recently, used the land for dairy herds. At present, saving only the large field to the east of the driveway to the house, most of these have the unkempt look of meadows no longer grazed. The grasses grow high and that blowsy yellow menace, ragwort, is all too apparent in them (its one saving grace being that a distinctive black and orange hooped caterpillar loves its toxins and, when it turns into the attractive red and black cinnabar moth, it is left well alone by birds for that reason). Fortunately the seeming neglect is only temporary, for the farms are in the process of rearing beef cattle instead and, by withholding fertilizers and pesticides, are returning the fields to unimproved grassland of the kind that could one day become species-rich flower meadows.

For the moment it is, in summer, the verges of the lanes and tracks between the fields that are thick with marjoram, vetch, poppies, agrimony, ladies bedstraw, self heal, scabious and even traveller's joy. As usual, where there are wild flowers there are insects and butterflies to take advantage of them and, with the woods encroaching on the fields, you are likely to see both the birds and the butterflies that like meadows, verges and woodland fringes. This is countryside that also conceals three of the mammals that live closest to human beings whilst we, more often than not, are completely unaware of them – badgers, deer and foxes. The preferred habitat for a badger's sett is within the edge of a wood with open fields nearby where, with its immensely powerful sense of smell it can sniff out its staple food, earthworms, 2 inches (5 cm) deep within the soil. Yet it will eat most things if push comes to shove, just like that arch scavenger, the red fox who, as we know, will scour our dustbins if necessary. Its eating habits may not meet with our fullest approval but its family life is almost blameless. Often, though not always, there are several females within a family group but only one male. In such circumstances only the senior female or females breed, but the spinster aunts all take part in looking after the cubs after birth.

Among the attractions of Stanmer Park is that the tracks leading upwards to the northern boundary of the estate link up with a network of paths across the South Downs and, as it goes almost without saying, the views are tremendous.

Hastings Country Park

It seems laughable to call Hastings Country Park an urban nature reserve but with its western end tucked into the town and suburban housing behind its first mile, that's what it is. It is a superb sweep of clifftop paths connecting deep glens, heath, meadows and ancient woodland, stretching over 5 miles (8 km), and offering staggering views. To the west the prow of Beachy Head thrusts into the sea, cradling Eastbourne in its lee; to the east, the Dungeness power station surfs outward on its shingle bed; and inland you look north west to the Weald or north east into Kent. Hastings Borough Council may get brickbats for the Queensway business park in Marline Valley, but it merits great praise for securing this reserve and encouraging its restoration.

One can think of the reserve's 660 acres (270 hectares) as being five interconnected areas, each with its own characteristics. Close to Hastings centre is East Hill. Then comes Ecclesbourne Glen, Fairlight Glen, Warren Glen and, finally, The Firehills, where the visitor centre stands not far from the prominent church tower. Deep Ecclesbourne Glen, a favourite haunt of smugglers in days gone by, is densely wooded with blackthorn, hawthorn and willow, shaped by the seasonal winds like extravagant swept-back hairstyles, but ideal for birds that live in scrub. It is also the home of many rare ferns, mosses, liverworts and lichens, making it a Site of Special Scientific Interest. Fulmars and redstarts breed on the spectacular clay and sandstone cliffs, as does the prince of prey birds, the peregrine, whose speed in the dive is unrivalled. Behind the cliffs are meadows waiting (at the time of writing) to be restored by regular cutting and grazing so that the soil is slowly rid of its too-rich nutrients and wild flowers return, bringing back seed-eating birds of the open field – linnets, sparrows, skylarks, song thrushes – and also short-eared owls and kestrels, our smallest bird of prey after the merlin, that hovers as it scours the grass for small mammals.

In Fairlight Glen there is ancient woodland, carpeted, in spring, with bluebells, yellow archangels, wood anemones, wild garlic and red campion. Yellow archangels look like dead nettles with circles of yellow flowers round the stems of the leaves, and wherever you come across them, you can be sure you are in woodland that has been undisturbed, maybe for generations.

Warren Glen is broader and more open than Ecclesbourne Glen as it slopes towards the sea, and in spring it is alive with the blues and yellows of bluebell and gorse. This is lowland heath, a rare habitat in itself but more uncommon still by being clifftop heath, of which there are few examples. Like other such sites, Warren Glen was overrun with bracken and the work of clearance is in its infancy, helped now by shaggy Highland cattle. Bracken is difficult to eradicate. Annual cutting slowly weakens its growth, but the old method was to trample it, bending the stems at their base with a crack that cuts off the sap – and this is what the cattle are doing. As the ground is gradually cleared, minotaur beetles dig in, literally. Their underground burrows contain a chamber reserved for the dung they scavenge on which their young can feed. It may not be the way you or I would raise our children, but baby minotaurs love it.

Minotaurs are among many unusual insects in the Park. There are sand-tailed digger wasps and tawny mining bees that make their homes in the soil. There is the beewolf (*Philanthus triangulum*), a rarity in Britain. The name suggests a voracious super-bee, something to duck if you see it coming, but in reality the boot is on the other foot. The beewolf is a wasp that paralyses bees, storing the living body for her larvae, but only after licking it with a bacterium that prevents decay through fungal growth. Another rarity is the purse-web spider (*Atypus affinis*), the only tarantula-like arachnid in Britain (but much smaller!) that waits for insects inside a tube-shaped web almost 1 foot (30 cm) in length.

The Firehills takes its name from the yellow gorse and purple-pink bell heather that it shares with Warren Glen, and that attracts winter visitors such as stonechats and Dartford warblers. In spring and autumn one must be prepared to spot unusual migrants anywhere over the reserve – two purple herons, for example, were spotted in early June 2007. But that is the beauty of wildlife reserves. Their occupants do not obey our rules and, on any given day, you can never be sure what you will be lucky enough to see.

Getting to Stanmer Park   National grid ref. TQ336094

❯ Off the A270 Brighton-Lewes road, just before it joins the A27(T) Brighton bypass.

Getting to Hastings Country Park   National grid ref. TQ859118

❯ On foot: from Roc-a-Nore Road via the East Cliff Railway.

❯ By car: there are three car parks: on Barley Lane for Ecclesbourne Glen; halfway along Fairlight Road for Fairlight Glen; and further east on Fairlight Road for The Firehills, Warren Glen and the Visitor Centre.

Acknowledgements

I owe grateful thanks to many people who have advised and encouraged me, and who have read and corrected each section from their own specialist knowledge of and close involvement with the sites I have written about. I wish to express my personal thanks and appreciation to (in alphabetical order) Chloe Bradbrooke, Rob Carver, Malcolm Emery, Caroline Fitzgerald, Alan Gillham, Peter Hughes, Mark Monk-Terry, Alice Parfitt, John and Margaret Pilkington, Adrian Thomas, Richard Williamson and Barry Yates; and in general to the Sussex Wildlife Trust who have been immensely helpful in advising and pointing out inaccuracies but have never sought to control the content in any way.

Last, but by no means least, I would like to record my appreciation of wildlife volunteers everywhere who give their time so willingly in helping to manage reserves. Most of all, though, I must mention my co-volunteers in the Trust's Conservation Hit Squad or, as we call ourselves, PRATS (pitchforkers, rakers and allied trades!). For what must seem to them like an age, they have had to put up with me asking questions and sometimes disappearing at moments of hard labour on the pretext of spotting some unusual specimen.

David Mortimer, 2008

WILDLIFE ORGANISATIONS

**Butterfly Conservation,
Sussex Branch**
www.sussex-butterflies.org.uk
memberships@sussex-butterflies.org.uk
branch@sussex-butterflies.org.uk

Natural England (Sussex)
Telephone 01273 476595
www.naturalengland.org.uk/regions
*enquiries.southeast@natural
england.org.uk*

**Royal Society for the
Protection of Birds**
South East Regional Office,
42 Frederick Place, Brighton
BN1 4EA
Telephone 01273 775333
southeast@rspb.org.uk

**Royal Society for the Protection
of Birds (Pulborough Brooks)**
Telephone 01798 875851
www.rspb.org.uk/reserves
pulborough.brooks@rspb.org.uk

Stanmer Park, Brighton
Telephone 01273 293080
parks@brighton-hove.gov.uk

Sussex Wildlife Trust
Woods Mill, Henfield,
West Sussex BN5 9SD
Telephone 01273 492630
www.sussexwt.org.uk

**West Sussex County Council
(Pagham Harbour)**
Pagham Harbour Visitor Centre,
Selsey Road, Sidlesham,
West Sussex PO20 7NE
Telephone 01243 641508
www.westsussex.gov.uk
pagham.nr@westsussex.gov.uk

**Chailey Common Local Nature
Reserve Management Committee**
East Sussex County Council,
County Hall, St Anne's Crescent,
Lewes BN7 1UE
Telephone 01273 482670

Chailey Commons Society
Telephone 01444 413716

Friends of Bedelands Farm
*Telephone 01444 236871 or
01444 242279*

Hastings Country Park
Telephone 01424 813225
www.wildhastings.org.uk

**Mid Sussex District Council
(Bedelands Farm)**
Telephone 01444 458166
www.midsussex.gov.uk
ParksOpenSpaces@midsussex.gov.uk

National Trust (Nymans Woods)
Telephone 01444 405250
nymans@nationaltrust.org.uk

OTHER SITES WORTH VISITING

West Sussex

West Dean Woods

2 miles (3 km) west of A286 Midhurst-Chichester road

The reserve itself is not open to the public but a public footpath runs along its north west edge. From it can be seen in spring a display of wild daffodils numbering, in a prolific year, some 2.5 million.

Amberley Wild Brooks

Accessed from the village of Amberley, west of Storrington

One of the country's most important bird sites, with an estimated 37,000 wintering waders and wildfowl. Its many drainage ditches contain 50 per cent of the species of the entire aquatic flora of Britain.

East Sussex

Bewl Water

Accessed off the B2099 road west of Wadhurst

Bewl Water is like an irregularly shaped, ragged tripod. The middle leg of the tripod has three large 'toes' and the wildlife reserve is between the second and third toe. The reserve is mainly concerned with birds, and among its specialities are little and great crested grebes.

Friston Forest

Accessed from southern end of Littlington road off A259

A large beech forest on what, until about 60 years ago was chalk downland. Deep underground are the aquifers that store Eastbourne's water, so the risk of pollution from fertilisers and chemicals meant the land could not be used for anything but trees and wildlife. There are many wildlife-rich openings, rides and clearings where chalk heath and downland meet the woods.

Urban nature reserves

Buchan Country park

Accessed from the westbound lane of the A264 Crawley-Horsham road

170 acres (70 hectares) of meadows, heath, woods and wetland two miles from Crawley town centre. The woodlands 'are stuffed with birds' according to the Senior Ranger, and roe deer are present in them. The two picturesque ornamental lakes of acidic water attract more than 20 species of dragonfly and kingfishers are sometimes seen over one of them, Douster Pond. The Park also contains a significant area of heath over which heather blooms, butterflies flutter and in which adders bask during summer.

INDEX